MEDITATION ON THE THRESHOLD

Bilingual Press/Editorial Bilingüe

General Editor
Gary D. Keller

Managing Editor
Karen S. Van Hooft

Senior Editor
Mary M. Keller

Assistant Editor
David C. Rubí D.

Editorial Board
Juan Goytisolo
Francisco Jiménez
Eduardo Rivera
Severo Sarduy
Mario Vargas Llosa

Address
Bilingual Review/Press
Hispanic Research Center
Arizona State University
Tempe, Arizona 85287
(602) 965-3867

MEDITATION ON THE THRESHOLD

ROSARIO CASTELLANOS

A Bilingual Anthology of Poetry
Translation & Introduction
by Julian Palley

Bilingual Press/Editorial Bilingüe
TEMPE, ARIZONA

© 1988 by Bilingual Press/Editorial Bilingüe

ISBN: 0-916950-80-8

Library of Congress Catalog Card Number: 87-73552

PRINTED IN THE UNITED STATES OF AMERICA

Cover design by FORMAZ

This publication is made possible, in part, with public funds from the New York State Council on the Arts.

Contents

Feminism in the Poetry of Rosario Castellanos

Gabriella de Beer

Rosario Castellanos (1925–1974) was an important writer of our time. Her voice speaks to us in many tones, and her message merits close study. Born after 1910 and brought up in that post-revolutionary environment which so profoundly influenced the literature and art of twentieth-century Mexico, she made valuable contributions to the novel, short story, theatre, essay, and poetry.[1] Castellanos was a multifaceted writer who created a solid body of writing, thus earning her a distinguished place in the letters of the continent. Her life was cut short at the height of her career through a household accident in Israel while serving as Mexican ambassador.

An overview of Rosario Castellanos' writings reveals that feminism as a theme is present in one form or another in the various genres that she practiced. In the three collections of short stories, *Ciudad Real* (1960), *Los convidados de agosto* (1964), and *Album de familia* (1971), as well as in her two novels, *Balún-Canán* (1957) and *Oficio de tinieblas* (1962), women and their place in a traditional and patriarchal world are central issues. It is perhaps in the essays of Rosario Castellanos where the feminist theme is most prevalent. The reader cannot help but notice the large number of articles and essays that deal with women as historical figures, writers, or simply spectators of the Mexican world dominated by men. This writer was plainly conscious of her position in a developing society and through her writing faced squarely the problems of women in a society that restricts them and casts them aside.[2]

The title of a collection of essays published posthumously (1979) proclaims its contents and underscores its theme. The book *Mujer que sabe latín . . .* immediately brings to mind the old saying which ends with the words "ni tiene marido ni tiene buen fin" ("A woman who

knows Latin has neither a husband nor will come to a good end").
These essays comprise Castellanos' strongest denunciation of the role
of women in Mexican and, hence, in Latin American society. In them
she gives her interpretation of the female role since biblical times to
the decade of the 70's. Not limiting herself to just outlining their situ-
ation, she speaks in favor of academic preparation for women and of
their right to enjoy all the opportunities that the world makes availa-
ble to men. In addition, Castellanos shares with her readers her
knowledge of and interest in feminist writers of world renown. A few
names will give a clear idea of her familiarity with the theme: Simone
Weil, Isak Dinesen, Virginia Woolf, Lillian Hellman, Clarice Lispec-
tor, and María Luisa Bombal among others. All of this as well as
Rosario Castellanos' own life are evidence of her clear comprehension
of the situation of women and her deep commitment to come to grips
with it and to suggest a future course of action.

It would not be excessive to say that Rosario Castellanos worked
on her poetry with greater literary consciousness than she did her prose.
In an interview with Emmanuel Carballo (1962) the writer reveals her
poetic development—her urge to write poetry, the poets that influenced
her, and the evolution of her techniques and themes.[3] When Carballo
asked her how she arrived at poetry and why she stayed with it, she
replied: "I arrived at poetry after convincing myself that the other paths
were not valid for survival. And at that time what interested me most
was survival. Poetic language constitutes the only way to achieve per-
manence in this world."[4] We can see, therefore, that Castellanos
chose poetry because she considered it the appropriate genre to achieve
what was valid and eternal. In studying the interview closely one is
drawn to the frankness of the writer and her strong self-criticism and
objectivity in judging her own work, characteristics uncommon among
young writers. Castellanos rejects *Trayectoria de polvo* (1948) and *Apuntes
para una declaración de fe* (1949)[5] as experimental, ill-conceived, and
rhetorical. It is not until the publication of *De la vigilia estéril* (1950)
that she feels that she has come close to creating her own style by em-
barking upon a poetic course that is personally satisfying. Curiously,
it is in this work that her concern with women appears if not as a main
theme, then as an underlying current. *De la vigilia estéril* was the result
of her search for a style midway between abstract and concrete. The
two sources of readings that most influenced both this collection and
El rescate del mundo (1952) were Gabriela Mistral and the Bible.

The mark of Gabriela Mistral is seen in all of Castellanos' poetry.

For, like Mistral, Castellanos is the poet of solitude and motherhood, of unrequited love of the simple woman, be she a peasant or a housewife, but always deserving of dignity and respect. The women depicted in her work are ethereal, sad, lonely, and forlorn; they suffer in silence surrounded by nature whose multiple manifestations reflect their mood. The "Elegías del amado fantasma" ("Elegies of the Phantom Lover," pp. 37–41) illustrate the tone and theme of this early poetry as well as the clear influence of Gabriela Mistral who, in many ways, is Castellanos' predecessor. The "Segunda elegía" ("Second Elegy") is a good example:

> I rock my pain to sleep like a mother her child
> or I take refuge in it like a child in his mother
> alternately possessor and possessed.
>
> I didn't know that afternoon
> that when I was saying goodbye you were saying death.
>
> Now it is not possible to know anything.
>
> To let my head drop exhausted
> I look for a smooth stone as a pillow.
> I only ask for an edge of loneliness and tedium
> to give shelter to my lost tenderness. (p. 39)

Of interest from the collection *El rescate del mundo* are the poems of the last section, "Diálogo con los oficios aldeanos" ("Dialogue with the Villagers' Crafts," pp. 66–68). They deal with washerwomen, coffee pickers, and weavers. In short, they depict simple women working at the village chores. Here Castellanos, using austere language, shows us her admiration and sympathy for the working woman. In "Escogedoras de café en el Soconusco" ("Coffee Pickers in the Soconusco") the poet identifies with her:

> With one hand they set aside
> the best grains,
> with the other they discard
> and weigh and measure.
> Wisdom walking
> in coarse garments.
> Would that I choose my steps
> as do you, justly. (pp. 66–67)

"Lamentación de Dido" ("Dido's Lament," pp. 93–97), a rather long composition in which the poet evokes the history of this classic figure to express her own sentiments, was published in *Poemas 1953–1955* (1957). Although on several occasions Rosario Castellanos had said that her poetry was not autobiographical, in speaking of "Lamentación de Dido" she did confess that with this poem she wished "to salvage an experience . . . through an image situated in the timeless, in tradition."[6] But of greater importance was her statement about the permanence of poetry. According to her, poetry, like philosophy, aspires to permanence. Therefore, love should be treated "as an essential phenomenon of human nature, and not as a mood that might last one or more minutes."[7]

In the years 1959 and 1960 during which the volumes *Al pie de la letra* and *Lívida luz* were published we see a tendency toward the prosaic in Rosario Castellanos' poetry. The two collections are about concrete subjects and people and composed in a style that is unrhetorical. *Lívida luz* marks the poet's passage from the world of esthetic contemplation to the real world of people of flesh and blood, capable of cruelty and brutality. The poem "Jornada de la soltera" ("Woman Alone," p. 175) is the lament of an unmarried woman who lives in a society in which marriage is normal and the unmarried state is abnormal. Anyone who chooses to be single suffers shame and anguish.

Materia memorable of 1969 appears almost a decade after the previous collection of poetry and after the publication of her two novels which were so well received.[8] In this collection of poetry Castellanos works with subjects dealt with earlier but with even greater simplicity and fewer images. In these poems she expresses very concrete ideas. The women depicted here are the lady of the house, the housewife, the mother, the working woman or farm laborer who has her traditional role in the home or the field. For example, in "Sobremesa" ("After Dinner") we see the woman who accepts her inferior position in the company of men.

> After dinner they remain a while
> around the table. There the men
> smoke their cigars; the women
> patiently labor at their needlework, whose beginning
> one hardly recalls. Black coffee gives off steam
> in cups often called for.
>
> Someone cuts the pages of a book

> or collects the bread crumbs between her fingers
> and the one over there tells of the months
> of her pregnancy to the one who has already raised her children.
>
> (p. 191)

In "Testamento de Hécuba" ("Hecuba's Testament," pp. 195–197) we see the hard-working woman, faithful wife, exemplary mother, and ultimately the lonely and abandoned widow. The virtuous woman of "Emblema de la virtuosa" ("Emblem of the Virtuous Woman," pp. 209–210) is also like the others—fated to be obedient, loyal, and alone. In "Acción de gracias" ("Thanksgiving," pp. 216–218) Castellanos speaks of her own background and her pride in a well-ordered house—clean clothes, prepared meals, shiny utensils—just as her mother had taught her by example. "My mother used to repeat: / patience is metal that shines" (p. 217). Traditionally these women have been lauded and admired by our history and culture. But of greater significance is the fact that women themselves have viewed their mothers as models of femininity. In an essay of Castellanos' "La participación de la mujer en la educación formal" ("The Participation of Women in Formal Education") she makes clear that this traditional role is no longer sufficient for women.[9]

Unquestionably, the most direct and forthright statements about women are in Rosario Castellanos' later poetry. There are no more classical or biblical allusions nor feminist concepts carefully veiled by images and metaphors. Here the writer's sytle and her use of poetic language have reached their full development. All that came before was an experiment, whereas her writing of the 70's marks her success and achievement as a feminist poet. This attitude is not new but the result of the evolution of her sytle and the encouragement drawn from the interest and frank treatment that feminism generated. In a revealing interview the poet speaks of her collection *Poesía no eres tú* (1972). Judging her own work from the perspective of both time and distance, she emphasizes the constancy of her ideas, the change in her poetic language, and the importance of anecodotal material. She concludes by saying: "Now I feel free to abandon the rules and to seek elsewhere something that is valid for me."[10] When Castellanos speaks of the women depicted in her books she stresses the one characteristic that unites them all—loneliness.

> My earliest experience was individual loneliness; soon
> I discovered that all the other women I knew were in

the same situation: single women alone, married wom-
en alone, mothers alone. Alone putting up with very
rigid customs that condemned love and lovemaking as
unforgivable sins. Alone in their idleness because that
was the only luxury their money could buy.[11]

En la tierra de en medio (1972) combines Castellanos' purest style with
her most direct and aggressive treatment of the feminist theme. Most
of the poems in this collection focus on women. Some are based on
an autobiographical event and others on a historical figure or happen-
ing. Of these "Malinche" (pp. 285–287), the Mexican symbol of the
repressed woman, is the most illustrative. But more typical are the
poems of a personal nature in which the writer, using her own ex-
periences, speaks for all women. In them biting humor and mocking
irony alternate with serious reflections. For example, in "Autorretra-
to" ("Self-portrait," pp. 288–290) Castellanos describes herself and
speaks of her career and daily routine. But she tells us also that she
suffers, that she is unhappy, and that she cries because that sort of
behavior is expected of her. Unfortunately, they also taught her to
cry about silly little things: "I cry when I burn the rice or when I lose
/ the latest receipt for the property taxes" (p. 290). And from that
recollection stems her bitterness. In like fashion, in "Economía domés-
tica" ("Domestic Economy," pp. 291–292) she shares with her readers
"the golden rule" taught to her by her mother and transmitted like a
legacy: "To have a place for everything / and to have / everything in
its place" (p. 291). She describes her house with every little thing in
its place and everything nice and clean and shiny. There are, she feels,
certain things that do not lend themselves to order such as weeping,
nostalgia, and grief. But despite experiencing these disconcerting emo-
tions the deeply ingrained golden rule always prevails:

> All this makes me uncomfortable. I always say:
> tomorrow . . .
> and then forget. And I proudly show off to my guests
> the sitting room where shines resplendent
> the golden rule inherited from my mother.   (p. 292)

The upbringing she had received was geared to the passive acceptance
of things as they occurred, meekness, and the lack of protest when
the situation called for just the opposite. We witness a continuous con-
flict between what Rosario Castellanos perceives as a woman's role

and the combined effect of her environment and upbringing that causes her to be submissive and subservient in a society ordered by men. It is perhaps in this inner struggle of wishing to be different by rebelling against a cultural tradition that we find her most outspoken feminism, rage, and nostalgia. Castellanos realizes that the road is arduous, the struggle to be as we wish difficult, and the weapons at hand insufficient. That is what brings about her anger and frustration.

Loneliness that so often appears in the poetry of Rosario Castellanos is alleviated by motherhood. In "Se habla de Gabriel" ("Talking about Gabriel," p. 291), a poem about the birth of her son, Castellanos describes how she felt while she was pregnant in terms understandable by any mother—"ugly, sick, bored"—and ends her work with a burst of satisfaction and fulfillment.

> I gave in. And through the opening from which he emerged
> through that
> tearing of his separation from me
> also went the last vestige that I had
> of loneliness, of my looking out from behind a glass. (p. 291)

Motherhood like writing constituted the opposite of loneliness, of nothingness, of "looking out from behind a glass." When in "Entrevista de prensa" ("Interview," pp. 293–294) a reporter asked her, "Why, to what purpose do you write?" she replied:

> I write because one day (I was an adolescent)
> I looked in the mirror and no one was there.
> Can you imagine? A void. And those
> around me gushed importance. (p. 293)

"Válium 10" (pp. 296–297) is very likely the most serious and most amusing poem in this collection. Here the speaker in describing a typical day in her life portrays the contemporary woman—mother, wife, homemaker, professional—harassed by the multiple responsibilities and demands of her life. This woman can't sleep without that pill "in which is condensed, / chemically pure, the world's order" (p. 297).

Otros poemas, a small collection whose style and language places it in the 70's, includes two poems that illustrate the poet's comprehension of the place of women and of how they are viewed by the modern world. In "Telenovela" ("Soap Opera," pp. 312–314) Castellanos is relentless with television, whose simple presence in the home resolves family arguments, erases class differences, and like a magnet draws

everyone to it. On the "Big Boob Tube" there parade women created
with those preconceived ideas that the public, conditioned by televi-
sion, wishes to see. Castellanos shows us women that we all recog-
nize, universal types—the nurse, the self-sacrificing widow, the
long-suffering sweetheart, the schemer, the single girl who has become
pregnant, and also those women who do mouthwash, detergent, and
deodorant commercials, products that "guarantee" beauty and happi-
ness.[12] These images provided by advertising and accepted by the
public—both male and female—are a caricature of reality. The poet
cannot but judge and condemn our culture in which one's most inti-
mate secrets are "under the jurisdiction of the advertiser" (p. 314). The
other poem is "Kinsey Report" (pp. 317–320) in which Castellanos uses
as her frame of reference the well-known report that in its day caused
such a sensation.[13] Writing in the first person, the poet depicts with
clever irony the different women studied in the Kinsey Report. One
by one they march by: the married woman, now somewhat heavier
than when she was a bride, who gives in to the amorous demands of
her husband out of obedience and at the same time resists them out
of "modesty"; the single woman who submits to men since it is expect-
ed of her and because she is lonely and without any illusions of mar-
riage; next comes the divorcée, followed by the woman who shuns sex
for religious reasons, and then the lesbian. And finally Castellanos ends
her poem with the young lady who awaits her "Prince Charming" who
will come one day and then they will live happily ever after just like
in the fairy tales. With a note of sarcasm Castellanos concludes that
despite Kinsey and the different norms of behavior he studied, it is
the average woman, the traditional one, the one who dreams of hap-
piness, the one who is faithful to the German saying that a woman's
role is to devote herself to her children, her kitchen, and her church,
who is typical in Mexico today.

Rosario Castellanos by example and through her writing has made
strong statements about today's women. Although she has insisted that
her poetry is not autobiographical, the attitudes expressed in it are
the result of her experiences as a professional, mother, wife, homemak-
er, and student of Mexican society. One can note in her work two
directions that reflect the situation of contemporary woman. On the
one hand, she is faithful to her upbringing and culture with whatever
virtues and defects may have gone into them. Her culture, as false
and outdated as it may be, is so deeply ingrained in her being that
she cannot cast it aside. On the other hand, Castellanos points out

that today's woman does have opportunities once exclusively reserved for men that are opening up avenues toward different life styles. The poet emphasizes that it is in the clash between tradition and modernity that her loneliness and anguish lie. Her very being, controlled by norms of behavior that were absorbed with her mother's milk, cannot yet free itself totally. And it is for this reason that the writer herself sometimes behaves as she is expected to, conforming to the classic model.

Rosario Castellanos understands the conflicts within the Mexican woman. Her poetry describes for us the way she lives, suffers, and dreams in the big cities and the rural towns. The writer's attitude is not pessimistic; it is, on the contrary, realistic. Knowing the problem and understanding its complexities thoroughly, she speaks out in support of education and culture free of sexist values. She encourages women to reject the "plastic" images created by the advertising media. But basically Rosario Castellanos' message is sobering: the full participation and acceptance of women in contemporary society is not yet assured. In order to reach this goal both men and women must change their attitudes and reject false standards. This transformation implies a change in the social order so as to allow women to assume their just places. Castellanos realizes that the road to achieve this goal is a long one and that the distance that has been covered and is still to be covered may not be advancing at a desired pace. However, one does come away from her poetry with the certainty that slowly but surely that goal will be reached.

THE CITY COLLEGE OF THE
CITY UNIVERSITY OF NEW YORK

Notes

[1] For a study of the techniques and themes in the poetry of Rosario Castellanos, see Maureen Ahern and Mary Seale Vásquez, eds., *Homenaje a Rosario Castellanos* (Valencia: Ediciones Albatros-Hispanófila, 1980); Germaine Calderón, *El universo poético de Rosario Castellanos* (México: UNAM, Centro de Estudios Literarios, 1979); Marcia Anne Bigelow, "La evolución de la hablante en la poesía de Rosario Castellanos," Diss. Univ. of California, Irvine 1983; also the "Selected Bibliography" compiled by Julian Palley at the end of this volume.

[2] For a study on feminism in the work of Rosario Castellanos, see Beth Miller, "El feminismo mexicano de Rosario Castellanos," in *Mujeres en la literatura* (México: Fleischer Editora, 1978), pp. 9–19.

[3] By this date her poetry consisted of seven small collections.

[4] Emmanuel Carballo, "Rosario Castellanos," in *Protagonistas de la literatura mexicana* (México: SEP, 1986), p. 520.

[5] Rosario Castellanos' poetry has been published in a single volume *Poesía no eres tú* (México: Fondo de Cultura Económica, 1972). All references to her poems are from this edition with corresponding page numbers indicated in parenthesis.

[6] Carballo, p. 524.

[7] Carballo, p. 524.

[8] The novels she published during these years are *Balún-Canán* (1957) and *Oficio de tinieblas* (1962).

[9] "The feminine ideal in Western culture (to which we, in large measure, are heirs) presents a series of constants that have hardly varied over time and from place to place. The strong woman as she appears in the Scriptures is so because of her maiden purity, her faithfulness to her husband, her devotion to her children, her industriousness in her home, and her care and prudence in managing the inheritance which she is not qualified to receive or own. Her qualities are loyalty, faithfulness, patience, chastity, submissiveness, modesty, discretion, unselfishness, self-sacrifice, and letting all her actions be governed by that evangelical precept that the last shall be first." In *Mujer que sabe latín . . .* (México: Sep Setentas Diana, 1979), pp. 21–22.

[10] Beth Miller and Alfonso González, "Rosario Castellanos," in *26 autoras del México actual* (México: B. Costa-Amic, 1979), p. 131.

[11] Miller and González, p. 135.

[12] This description of today's woman reminds us of Octavio Paz's characterization of women in his essay "Máscaras mexicanas" in *El laberinto de la soledad* (1950).

[13] Alfred Charles Kinsey (1894–1956) published two studies on sexual behavior that created a sensation at the time: *Sexual Behavior of the Human Male* (1948) and *Sexual Behavior of the Human Female* (1953).

I wish to thank the Fondo de Cultura Económica and the estate of Rosario Castellanos for permission to use the poems from *Poesía no eres tú*.

No one achieves salvation alone, Sartre has said. And the day we may find a genuinely praiseworthy woman it will be because the factors which obstruct her appearance no longer exist: the tyrant and his oppressed nation, the opulent and the beggar, the executioner and the victim. When they [the men] will also have become genuinely worthy of respect.

Rosario Castellanos, from a review of Mercedes Valdivieso's *La brecha,* in *El uso de la palabra,* p. 39.

PREFACE

I was in Mexico City in the fall of 1974, reading *Balún Canán*, Rosario Castellanos' novel of her childhood in Chiapas, when I heard about her absurd, tragic death in Tel Aviv. She had been appointed Mexican ambassador to Israel two years earlier, and died in an accident in the embassy.

I began soon after to read her poetry, collected in a work with the curious title of *Poesía no eres tú*, "Poetry Thou Art Not" (also the title of a poem). Hers was — it seemed to me then and even more so now — a profoundly original voice in Mexican poetry. In what are, for me, her best poems, she speaks directly, in a colloquial idiom, of the ironies and tragedies of being a gifted intellectual woman in contemporary Latin America.

Rosario Castellanos was born in Mexico City in 1925, but at an early age she moved, with her family, to the southern state of Chiapas, where she spent her childhood and adolescence. She lived close — physically and psychologically — to the Chiapas Indians, of Mayan origin; her childhood, and the conflicts between the Indians and the *ladinos* (Spanish-speaking Mexicans) are portrayed in her novels and short stories. She returned to Mexico City to study at the National University, where she became known for her wit and intellect, joining a circle of emerging young writers — among them, Sergio Magaña, Jaime Sabines, Luisa Josefina Hernández, Emilio Carballido, Ramón Xirau and Rubén Bonifaz Nuño — who were to form part of an important literary generation. After a year at the University of Madrid, in 1950, she spent several years in her native Chiapas, first as director of cultural activities for the Instituto de Ciencias y Artes, and later as director of the regional guignol theater. These adult years in Chiapas were crucial for the development of her art, and she said later that "My two years in San Cristóbal has been one of the most important experiences of my life" (Poniatowska, 1958, p. 7). She taught for several years at the Facultad de Filosofía y Letras at the National University, until a political intervention in 1966, forcing the removal of a popular rector, Ignacio Chávez, obliged her to resign in protest. Before her appointment as Mexican ambassador to Israel in 1971, she held visiting

professorships at the Universidad Iberoamericana in Mexico City and
at several universities in the United States. She married the philosopher
Ricardo Guerra, and had one child, Gabriel. During her last years
in Israel she wrote a play, *El eterno femenino*, a brilliant denunciation
of middle-class mores, which was performed posthumously in 1976.
When her body was returned from Israel in 1974, she was accorded
a national funeral, and buried in the *Rotonda de los hombres ilustres* (the
Pantheon of Famous Men).

Poesía no eres tú (1972) contains all the poetry published during her
lifetime (with the exception of early poems she did not wish to reprint),
a total of 180 poems. Included also are translations from Emily Dick-
inson, St.-John Perse and Paul Claudel, two plays in verse ("Salomé"
and "Judith") and glosses on well-known Spanish and Latin Ameri-
can poets. For this anthology I have chosen forty-three from the 180
of *Poesía no eres tú*. Her first collections are sparsely represented here,
while the majority are taken from *Al pie de la letra* (1959), *Lívida luz*
(1960), *Materia memorable* (1969), *En la tierra de en medio* (1972) and *Otros
poemas* (1972). The poems are in chronological order (that is, accord-
ing to the dates of her books), except for the first, "Meditation on the
Threshold", and the last, "Request."

I would like to thank Raúl Ortiz y Ortiz, a close friend and execu-
tor of the will of Rosario Castellanos, for serving as a true Virgil in
my discovery of her writings. I am indebted to several persons, in-
cluding some anonymous readers, for suggestions regarding the trans-
lations. My special thanks to Professor Myriam Díaz-Diocaretz, of
the University of Concepción (Chile), who worked with me in improv-
ing the tone and accuracy of these versions. My thanks also to Mar-
cia Anne Bigelow for some suggestions that arose during the writing
of her dissertation on Castellanos. I would like to express my grati-
tude to Gary D. Keller and the editors of the Bilingual Press for their
encouragement and recommendations during the revision of this
manuscript. Finally, I am grateful for the opportunity to include an
essay by Gabriella de Beer which was originally published in Spanish
in the *Revista de Crítica Literaria Latinoamericana* (Lima). A few notes
are appended at the end of the anthology, which deal with problems
of translations or with socio-historical circumstances that may not be
familiar to the English-speaking reader.

JULIAN PALLEY
UNIVERSITY OF CALIFORNIA, IRVINE

Introduction

Rosario Castellanos: Eros and Ethos

> Telling the truth about one's own body: a necessary,
> freeing subject for the woman writer.
>   Tillie Olsen, *Silences*

> The boldness of exploring one's self; the need to be-
> come conscious of one's bodily existence or the
> unheard-of pretension to confer a meaning on one's
> spiritual existence are severely repressed and punished
> by the social apparatus. The latter has proclaimed, once
> and for all, that the only legitimate attitude of femi-
> ninity is that of waiting.
>   Rosario Castellanos, *Mujer que sabe latín* . . . p. 14.

Rosario Castellanos' late poetry,[1] the kind that is prominent in this anthology, speaks to us, at times with considerable candor, of the inner problems of anguished sexuality and love, while at the same time it projects and decries the subordinate situation of women in the structures of Latin American society. Of course, inevitably, the inner demands and the repressions of the symbolic order, or society, form part of the same interacting and complex relationship. The struggle between the inner demands and the outer repression becomes the principal theme of her best poetry; one that, I submit, no other Latin American poet has dealt with with such honesty, depth and creative mastery. At the same time, that theme is transcended by a general existential and social compassion. In the following pages I will be examining several aspects of the poetry of Castellanos: feminism, alienation, desire, style and her use of the dramatic monologue.[2]

Feminism and Social Criticism

Much of Castellanos' considerable literary production—poetry, novels, short stories, essay and theater—shows a feminist posture of criticism of the role and treatment of women in contemporary Mexican society. "Sobre cultura femenina" ("On Feminine Culture") was the title of her Master's Thesis presented in 1950 to the National Univer-

nalist and novelist Elena Poniatowska called it the "point
- departure for the contemporary women's movement in Mexico."[3]
"The thesis," wrote Mary Seale Vásquez,

> explores the reasons for the lack of female cultural par-
> ticipation, finding that the terms in which such activi-
> ty was carried out in a male dominated culture were
> alien to women who sought permanence, not in a work
> of art, but in motherhood.[4]

Since that time, and until her death in 1974, Castellanos had become
the leading spokeswoman for Mexican feminism. A collection of es-
says on feminism and feminists, *Mujer que sabe latín . . . (Woman who
knows Latin . . .)*[5] appeared in 1973, with essays on Simone Weil, Vir-
ginia Woolf, Eudora Welty, Mary McCarthy and Betty Friedan,
among others.

In poetry, her feminist protest, usually ironic, takes several forms.
Her anger at the inferior status of women and their lack of recogni-
tion in Mexican society (a motif of her novel *Balún Canán*) appears
in such poems as "Interview" and "Ninguneo." The sexual role of wom-
an vis-à-vis man and the hypocrisy that this situation begets is manifest
in "Kinsey Report," while the tragedy of sexual and emotional depri-
vation is portrayed in "Woman Alone." The enslavement (conscious
or unconscious) to household and kitchen (see also her splendid story
"Lección de cocina," "Cooking Lesson") and the vexations of divided
responsibilities between home and work are delineated in "Valium 10"
and "Domestic Economy." Sexuality and love, and their frustrations,
emerge in "Small Chronicle" and "Nymphomania"; while the paradoxes
and impossibilities of marriage are apparent in "Game of Chess." A
cool, ironic image of herself, which includes tragicomic reflections on
being a middle class, intellectual woman in Mexico, is the subject of
"Self-Portrait." Most of these poems will be discussed in the course
of this essay.

We find in her work a frank and courageous confrontation with the
hypocrisies, the veiled power-struggle and woman's victimization and
suffering that prevail in Mexican society and generally in that of La-
tin America. Yet Castellanos was a feminist who did not employ the
angry rhetoric that we are accustomed to hearing from some Ameri-
can feminists. As Benoîte Groult said about the French feminists,[6]
she is capable of laughing at herself and placing herself in an ironic
perspective. She does not look upon the Other as the enemy, but seeks

reconciliation and liberation for both sexes; this is how I read the message of "Meditation on the Threshold," which ends with the line "Another kind of being, free and human." There is also social criticism of a general nature, unrelated to feminist concerns, in, for example, the poems about the suffering of the Indians in Chiapas in *El rescate del mundo*, as well as in such poems as "The Other" (about the solidarity the poet feels with the poor and the victims of social aggression) and "Memorial of Tlatelolco," which is concerned with the massacre of student protestors by government troops in Mexico City in 1968.[7]

"Woman does not exist."

In Luce Irigaray's dialogues with Lacan, whom she alternately affirms and ridicules, she plays with the assertion that in our phallocentric society, in our essentially masculine discourse, woman has no place.

> What is in excess in relation to form — such as the feminine sex (organ) . . . being necessarily rejected as beneath or beyond the system presently in effect. "Woman does not exist." In both *Encore* and *Télévision* Lacan repeatedly asserts that "woman does not exist." Discursivity, the reigning system, cannot include woman, because it demands the solid, the identical to the exclusion of the fluid. "Nonetheless the woman creature, it speaks . . . It speaks 'fluid.' " Hysterical speech, formless and useless like the discharges of the womb . . . ![8]

The "fluidity" of woman's discourse (and body) is a motif to be found in Castellanos' late poetry. In "Passport," for example, the speaker refers to herself as

> Woman, then, of a word. No, not of a word.
> Rather, of words.
> Many, contradictory, insignificant,
> pure sound, vacancy sprinkled with arabesques,
> parlor games, gossip, froth, forgetfulness.

Does the author speak of herself or of woman in general? The "fluidity" of the body is present also. In Lacanian theory, which was built

upon Freud, man suffers loss and separation from the mother's body
or breasts (which in his terminology is called the *objet petit a*); with man
and woman eternally seeking that lost object, sexuality is doomed to
failure. "Now, according to Irigaray, the object *a* refers back to a fluid
state 'Milk, luminous flow, acoustic waves . . . not to mention the gases
that are inhaled, emitted, differently perfumed, urine, saliva, blood,
plasma itself, etc.' "[9] So Lacan and Irigaray relate woman's "fluid"
economy to the amorphousness of her discourse. Man represents the
solid, the phallic. In Castellanos' "Small Chronicle" it is the fluids that
she most remembers from her love experience, fluids that cannot be
captured in mere ink, which "comes to us / from such a distant source."
Among the fluids, there was the blood of a torn hymen and

> The monthly hemorrhage or that in which
> a child says yes, says no to life.
> And the vein
> —mine or another's, what's the difference?—
> into which the suicidal edge plunges
> perhaps deeply enough to turn
> one into a death notice.
>
> There were, perhaps, other humors:
> the sweat of work, that of pleasure,
> anger's green secretion,
> semen, saliva, tears.

The speaker in many of Castellanos' poems sees herself as a non-
being, a non-entity; that is, as thus having been perceived and fixed
since childhood by the dominant phallocentric culture. This concep-
tion of herself is most clearly delineated in "Interview," although it
is suggested throughout her poetry:

> The reporter asks, with the customary shrewdness
>   of his profession:
> "Why, to what purpose do you write?"
>
> "Well, sir, it's obvious. Because someone
> (when I was a small girl)
> said that persons like myself do not exist.
> Because their bodies cast no shadow,
> because they register no weight on the scale,
> because their names are to be forgotten . . .

> "I write because one day (I was an adolescent)
> I looked in the mirror and no one was there . . ."

It is significant that the interviewer is a man, the sort of man, it may be assumed, who wonders why women do anything except stay at home and raise children. Later in the poem she "discovered / the power of the word" with which she asserted herself in the masculine world, and even left a few "corpses." Nevertheless, "love, happiness, / whatever . . ." were never "viable." She emerged from her non-being through art, through writing; although that was not enough to bring happiness and fulfillment. And she converted her "fetus" into a poem "from the book you'll one day praise." Fulfillment as artist and as feminist has had its price.

The subject's non-being in "Ninguneo" is political; that is, to the nothingness which resulted from her living in a phallocentric society, is added the workings of political assassination, or at least, of co-opting:

> A sentence which states: "You do not exist."
> Signed by those who employ the regal We;
> the One that is All; the magistrates,
> chancelleries, the major contracting parties,
> the Thirteen Aztec Emperors, the judicial
> and legislative branches, the list
> of Viceroys, the Boxing Commission,
> the Decentralized Colleges,
> The Single Union of Newspaper Hawkers, . . .
> . . . . . and, out of solidarity, the rest of
> my countrymen.

So we have a humorous litany of masculine authority, of the *nom-du-père* that dates back to the Aztec Emperors, which has condemned her to non-being. But in this case her non-being can be related to a specific historical event. When a popular rector of the National University was fired for political reasons, Castellanos resigned, along with a large number of her colleagues; but her opposition to the regime was absorbed and co-opted when she was subsequently made Ambassador to Israel. This is most likely the circumstances of this poem.

The non-being of the unmarried woman in "Woman Alone," is more acute, more tragic. The married woman, although marginated, at least fulfills herself, partially, with home and children. The unmarried woman, in the author's society, has no possible fulfillment; her very existence is "shameful." Her work is "without merit and without issue":

> She cannot be born in her child, in her womb,
> nor can she die in her remote and unexplored body,
> a planet whose existence
> the astronomer has only surmised,
> existing, although invisible.

Other Forms of Alienation: Woman as Object of Barter

Lévi-Strauss sees exogamy and the exhange of women between groups as one of the fundamental causes of the formations of human societies.[10] The French anthropologist sees the prohibition of endogamy not so much through fear of incest as the need for man to possess the *other*, that which is outside his immediate group; and woman was considered (and still is, in many circumstances — see Unamuno's novelette *Nada menos que todo un hombre*) an object, a possession that is exchanged among men like other possessions. One of the main thrusts of the feminist movement has been to struggle against the reification of woman. This alienation has not only to do with society's structures, but also with male sexual drives which tend to focus upon woman as object; the societal structures undoubtedly reflect the sexual attitudes.

In many of Castellanos' poems, the reification of woman, the use of woman as barter, is implicitly or explicitly condemned. From the legend of Malinche to the quasi-autobiographical "Reminder," the poet keeps returning to this theme. Malinche's mother, the queen, out of desire to please her new husband, pretends that the girl is dead; in reality she is sold into slavery, from which she will ultimately be given as a gift to Hernán Cortés.

> Such was the weeping and lamentation
> over an anonymous corpse; a cadaver
> that was not mine, because I, sold to
> the merchants, went forth into exile like a slave,
> a pariah.

"Reminder" appears to have a contemporary setting, although it conveys the idea of a repetition of primitive customs in a modern milieu:

Gentlemen: I obeyed your orders.

I bowed on entering,
I danced the adolescent dances,
and then sat down to wait for the arrival of the Prince.

Some approached me with the smug,
astute gesture of the horsedealer;
others calculated my weight
to judge the sum of my dowry
and another confided in his finger's touch
to learn the warp of my internal organs.

There was an intermediary between me and my body
an interpreter—Adam, who gave me the name
of woman that I now bear—
tracing in space the figure
of a forking delta.

Ah, destiny, destiny.

I have paid the tribute of my species
because I gave the earth, the world, that child
by which it is nourished and glorified.

It's time to approach the shore,
to return to the inner patios,
to extinguish the torches
because the task has been accomplished.

However, I still remain in my place.

Gentlemen, have you forgotten
to order my withdrawal?

The "Gentlemen" of the first line stresses the patriarchalism under the which the speaker lives in Mexican society, *le nom-du-père* of Lacan, who puns on the French *nom* (name) and *non* (no, negation). In this dramatic monologue, both the speaker and the time are only vaguely identified. The time could be precolumbian or the perspective could be contemporary with figurative or metaphorical allusions to primitive practices. Lines 2–4 suggest how the young girl early learns her "place" in society, how she must conform to rituals, and must passively await the arrival of the male, the prospective mate. The process of reification is accentuated grotesquely with the references to horse-dealing: "others calculated my weight"—as she compares herself to an animal put up for sale. "There was an intermediary between me and my body," the speaker affirms in the fourth strophe. The allusion is to the androcentric structures that were initiated, in our cultural heritage, in the book of Genesis, in which Adam was the first created and therefore privileged being. The speaker is not a free subject; she was created and named—given her identity—by the masculine God and by man, the other. The "forking delta," the child-bearing role assigned to her by a patriarchal God and by Adam, leads to the implicit association of anatomy with destiny (in the celebrated phrase), and the ironic reflection of "Ah, destiny." What the speaker does not state, in the silences, the spaces between lines and the strophes, is her innermost thoughts on the famous equation, thoughts that we may only guess at. Is woman as free as man to make her own future and destiny, or is she to be forever subject to the curse of the expulsion from paradise? But she has "paid her tribute," she has fulfilled that destiny; she has made the sacrifice or apotheosis of childbirth. Having done so, she is waiting for further orders from the *nom-du-père*, who has apparently forgotten her now that she has completed her assigned mission. She remains, in existential terms, shipwrecked, set adrift, perhaps *de trop*.

The margination of "Agony from Without the Walls" relates again to the sexual division of society; but here the female speaker looks with amazement, uncomprehending, at the predatory and prideless male animal who "smiles" and "half-opens his eyes" as he commits atrocious and selfish acts. If the oft-quoted masculine view is that woman is not quite human, we have here a reversal of perspective; it is the woman, the speaker, who looks with unbelief at man's actions, as of one from "some far shore, another region" ("de alguna orilla, de otra parte").[11] Man is a puzzling and different species. He "makes" the world, sweats, cohabits, steals, lies. He is driven by a need, a hunger, that is "harder than metal". The myths of the "passive" woman and the "active" man were created by the historical and prehistorical division of labor, and the need, now outmoded, for woman to spend much of her life in child-bearing and nurturing. But Castellanos sees this double standard from the deeper recesses of her psyche; she senses in the male a fundamental difference, a fierce need for action and predation, which may be motivated (although she does not say so) by womb envy, by man's unconscious knowledge that he cannot create life as woman can, and the resulting tendency to overcompensate for this lack in external activity.[12] In this, one of her most bitter and "feminist" poems, Castellanos wonders both at man's insensitivity and at her arrested ability to react positively to it, the slow death of which the speaker is witness.[13]

Desire

> Desire persists as an effect of primordial absence and it therefore indicates that, in this area, there is something fundamentally impossible about satisfaction itself. It is this process that, to Lacan, lies behind Freud's statement that "We must reckon with the possibility that something in the nature of sexual instinct itself is unfavorable to the realisation of complete satisfaction."
> Juliet Mitchell, *Feminine Sexuality*, p. 6.

In the remarkably frank language of "Small Chronicle," "Nymphomania" and "Kinsey Report" we perceive a world of woman's desire that is never fully realized, that is ultimately frustrated. Freud and Lacan do not, of course, limit this view of desire to the feminine; it is in the nature of the sexual drive that between the demand, the desire and the object there is a gap, a vacancy that is never bridged.[14] The "primordial absence," in Lacan's thinking, is that of the initial separation from the mother's body. Upon entering the symbolic order, the subject is separated both from the mother and from the "real," the indefinable unconscious.[15]

In "Small Chronicle" the juxtaposition of the blood of suicide along with the catalog of the "humors" of lovemaking suggests the need of desire along with its want, its lack. In a like manner, the various unfulfilled lives of "Kinsey Report" reveal the malfunctioning of sexual relationships within a given society, but they also hint at the ultimate impasse of desire itself, seen, of course, from the feminine point of view. Especially in "Nymphomania" we are presented with several metaphorical levels of unsatisfied desire:

> I had you in my grasp:
> all of humanity in a nutshell.
>
> What a hard and wrinkled rind!
>
> And within, the simulacrum
> of the two cerebral hemispheres

which, obviously, do not aspire to act upon
but to be devoured, lauded
for that neutral flavor, so unsatisfactory,
which demands of the infinite
to be tasted again and again, yet once more.

This is a poem that lends itself well to the reader response theories
of Umberto Eco and Wolfgang Iser. Each reader will see something
different in it; the "two cerebral hemispheres" are a polysemic symbol
that suggests a number of interpretations. The title itself seems to im-
ply the male genitals; but other signs in the poem ("the neutral flavor")
point to the nut that she mentions in the second line. And although
the object is only a "simulacrum" of the cerebral hemispheres, yet the
speaker could also refer to the brain itself and its insatiability, com-
paring the mind's activity to the sexual drive.

The nut, the brain and the testicles are characterized by this divi-
sion into two spheres or hemispheres; the desire the poem refers to
could be for food, for knowledge, or for the sexual object; in any case,
it is insatiable, it demands "to be tasted again and again." *"Encore* [La-
can's text] calls for both a repetition of the phallic performance, and
for something else. . . .[16] The poem moves rapidly between these var-
ious levels of meaning, at times suggesting knowledge (line 1), then
the nut or the genitals ("What a hard and wrinkled rind!"), then the
brain again in the third stanza, and concludes with ambiguous refer-
ences to either eating or sexual activity. It is a desire which exists in
fantasy but which can never attain the lost object.

Style: "to write what cannot be written."

In Jan Mukarovsky's study of "Poetic Designation,"[17] after expand-
ing on Bühler's categories of the functions of language (the presenta-
tional, the expressive and the appelative) to include the aesthetic, which
pertains only to poetic language, he goes on to conclude that symbol-
ic and figurative poetry, which reached its maximum expression in
the twenties, will now be replaced by a more direct and non-figurative
diction: "After a period in which imagery has been emphasized, there
can follow a period in which literal meaning will be stressed, not in
order to exchange one extreme for another but in order to reach a
synthesis through contradiction."[18] Mukarovsky thus foresaw those
trends which largely dispense with metaphor and symbol to achieve
a direct communication (anti-poetry, realism, the colloquial), a ten-

dency which can be already discerned in William Carlos Williams, during the twenties and thirties, and in such "anti-poets" as Nicanor Parra in Chile, Gloria Fuertes in Spain and Efraín Huerta in Mexico. In Mexico Salvador Novo, who belonged to an earlier generation, and Castellanos' contemporary Jaime Sabines have also employed, on occasion, a colloquial and ironic style. Mukarovsky saw the need for this direct poetic language, and understood the risks involved in its creation: "Today the risk, the necessary risk, of poetry consists much less in finding a new image—for the paths have already been trod and are entirely accessible to epigones—than in achieving a poetic designation of any kind which has a convincing relation to the reality designated."[19]

Poetic or aesthetic language—that of poetry—involves the intentional creation of a work that embodies a certain structure and unity, and that communicates an emotion. This recent poetry does not need the embellishments of rhyme, meter or imagery to create its effect, to move the reader. The aesthetic transaction is often achieved through what Viktor Shklovsky called "Defamiliarization," or the use of ordinary language in an unfamiliar way.[20] This tendency is apparent in contemporary Spanish poets like Angel González and Claudio Rodríguez; González compares hope to a spider in one poem, and Rodríguez, in another, begins to talk about "his shirt hung up to dry" but ends up talking about his soul. It is a strategy that allows the poet to dispense with usual accoutrements of poetry without sacrificing the poem's aesthetic impact.[21] The act of defamiliarization is perhaps always present in a successful poem; common language, or a metaphor, or a combination of images (as in surrealism), are "defamiliarized" to shock the reader into a new perception of reality. In Rosario Castellanos the defamiliarization consists not so much in the juxtaposition of unfamiliar motifs and images (as in González and Rodríguez), as it does in the break with the reader's expectations of how a twentieth century Mexican woman should write; she "should write" with gushing emotions and sensuous imagery (like, for example, Guadalupe Amor), and certainly not with the sudden and stark appearance of sexual realities on the white page:

> There were, perhaps, other humors:
> the sweat of work, that of pleasure,
> anger's green secretion,
> semen, saliva, tears.
> (from "Small Chronicle")

Or in "Kinsey Report," a poem which utilizes "clinical" descriptions
of the sexual activities of women from various strata of society, a
middle-class married woman explains some of her objections to the
sexual act:

> Besides, I'm concerned about another pregnancy.
> And the loud panting and the creaking of the bedsprings
> may wake up the children . . .

But even more than these candid confrontations with sexual matters,
Castellanos, as we shall see presently, "defamiliarizes" poetic language
itself by rejecting the given and inherited norms of such language,
norms that were fashioned by a masculine tradition.

We may discern in the evolution of Castellanos' poetry a movement
away from the metaphoric and the traditionally "poetic" to the direct
and unadorned statement, an original diction, which still conveys an
emotion to the reader. In her late poems, she speaks in a colloquial
idiom that both imitates natural speech and goes beyond it, employ-
ing an irony that masks a revolt against the enslavements and hypocri-
sies of society. The metaphor is not entirely absent from these poems,
but it is subdued, in the background, hardly noticeable. Her direct
speech, which surely shocked some readers by its candor, can be viewed
as part of an effort by woman writers of the West to free themselves
from the constraints of a male dominated, "phallic" language that con-
tinues the traditions of symbolism (for example, the poetry of Octa-
vio Paz). In these late poems (such as "Valium 10," "Self-Portrait,"
"Small Chronicle," "Kinsey Report," and "Domestic Economy"), her
style is characterized by the direct language of conversation, a tonali-
ty that changes with each poem (irony, sarcasm, compassion), the dra-
matic monologue and the frequent change of persona or poetic speaker,
and, as to form, free verse and the natural rhythm of breathing.
Although the metaphor is rare, at times its presence is a key to the
structure of the poem. For example, in "Domestic Economy," the im-
peccable order of the household is the "vehicle" (in I.A. Richards' terms)
which points to the "tenor": the intangibles that were lost or forgot-
ten: a sorrow, a nostalgia, a desire, or "remnants of time lost along
the way." This poem therefore tends toward the allegorical. So also,
in "Valium 10," there are two quasi-metaphors which illustrate the
poem's theme: the "insoluble crossword puzzle" that represents a lost
cosmic order; and the pill which creates, contains or returns (in an
illusory manner) that order.

Castellanos' early poetry (approximately from 1948 to 1959) may be characterized as "feminine" with the traditional connotations of overflowing sentiment, subjectivity, a narcissistic absorption in self, as well as, with regard to style, a flowing rhetoric that is traditionally "poetic" in its sonority and its search for the beautiful metaphor. We may take as an example the first three and the last three lines of "En el filo del gozo" ("On the Edge of Joy,"1948), which in many ways is a successful poem, although so removed from her later manner:

Entre la muerte y yo he erigido tu cuerpo:
que estrellen en ti sus olas funestas sin tocarme
y resbale la espuma deshecha y humillada.

. . . .

Y amor, cuando regresas
el ánimo turbado te presiente
como los ciervos jóvenes la vecinidad del agua.
               (*PNET*, pp. 31, 32)

(Between Death and Me I have raised up your body:
let its baneful waves break on you, without touching me,
and slip away into humbled and melted foam . . .
And, love, when you return,
may the troubled soul sense your coming
like the deer the region of water.)

In 1959, with *El pie de la letra*, Castellanos begins to discover her woman's voice that frees itself from both masculine models (symbolism, surrealism) and the usual kind of subjective style that is associated with most Latin American woman poets (with the exception, of course, of the Argentine Alfonsina Storni). She overturns "male" rhetoric with poems like "Two Meditations":

Little man, what would you do with your reason?
Bind up the world, the mad and furious world?
Castrate the colt called God?

(*Hombrecito*—little man—recalls Storni's *hombre pequeñito*, a feminist attack on man). The ordered view of the world, male and phallic, is here challenged by the implicitly feminine, intuitive, unconscious woman's vision, but utterly without sentimentality or rhetoric. She "deconstructs" the masculine symbolic order: "Though necessarily working within 'male' discourse, women's writing (in this scheme) would work

ceaselessly to deconstruct it; to write what cannot be written."[22]
Later, with *Lívida luz* (1960) and the volumes included in *Poesía no eres
tú* (1972), she would fully realize, achieve the mastery of a style that
is at once hard and humorous, uncompromising, ironic and unsen-
timental. "In the same way, the moment of desire (the moment when
the writer most clearly installs herself in her writing) becomes a refusal
of mastery [that is, of achieving "male" mastery], an opting for open-
ness and possibility, which can itself make women's writing a challenge
to the literary, structures it must necessarily inhabit."[23] In her last
books, Castellanos indeed "installs herself in her writing," and
"challenges the literary structures." Speaking of her later style, in which
she "begins to recognize her own voice," Castellanos herself remarks,
with her usual self-deprecation:

> Many of them [the late poems] are vulgar and obscene
> [*groseras*]. What's to be done about it? They serve to
> say what must be said. Nothing important or transcen-
> dent. Some glimpses of the structure of the world, the
> discovery of some coordinates to situate myself within
> it, the mechanics of my relationships with other beings.
> That which is neither sublime nor tragic. Perhaps, a
> little ridiculous.
>
> (*Mujer que sabe latín*, p. 207)

The Dramatic Monologue

The dramatic monologue in poetry may be defined as a first-person
voice which gradually develops the history, anecdotes and character
of the speaker, who takes on an existence which is usually indepen-
dent from that of the author. It was known to medieval literature, and
its most successful realization in English are undoubtedly those of
Robert Browning. The monologue usually implies a listener, a receiver;
the speaker of the monologue seems attentive to the listener's reac-
tions, and an implied or unspoken dialogue usually occurs. "Despite
its limitations to a single speaker, the monologue naturally assumes
a dramatic character. For vocalization itself craves an object—one or
many persons who constitute an audience. Thus the audience as well
as the speaker becomes a part of the total area of imagination."[24]

In this the monologue differs from the lyric poem in first person,
which is not necessarily directed to an audience and does not seek to
develop a round portrait of the speaker.

The first-person poem which tends toward the dramatic monologue appears early in the poetry of Rosario Castellanos. The richly metaphoric, yet abstract language of "Trayectoria del polvo" ("Trajectory of dust," 1948), in a style which the author would later abjure, tells a long and diffuse story of frustrated adolescence:

> Recuerdo: caminaba por largos corredores
> desbordantes de palmas y espejos.
> Yo, sedienta de mí, me detenía en estatuas
> duplicando el instante fugitivo en cristales ·
> y luego reiniciaba mi marcha de Narciso
> ya entonces como alada
> liberación de imagen entre imágenes.
> *(PNET,* p. 20)

> (I remember; I walked through long corridors
> overflowing with palms and mirrors.
> I, thirsty for myself, stopped before statues,
> duplicating the fleeing instant in glass
> and then began again my Narcissus walk
> now almost a winged
> liberation of image among images.)

This style, which has not yet attained the fullness of the dramatic monologue that Castellanos was to discover later, is continued in "En el filo del gozo" ("On the Edge of Joy," 1950) and "De la vigilia estéril" ("Of the Sterile Vigil"). These poems, although in the first person, are immersed in a subjective lyricism that does not coalesce into the portrait. It develops further in the *Dos Poemas* (*Two Poems*) of 1950, in which the author appears as a personage of the poem, an example of interior duplication:

> Yo no tendré vergüenza de estas manos vacías
> ni de esta celda hermética que se llama Rosario.
> En los labios del viento he de llamarme
> árbol de muchos pájaros.
> *(PNET,* p. 56)

> (I'll not be ashamed of these empty hands
> nor of this hermetic cell called Rosario.
> On the lips of the wind I will be named
> the Tree of Many Birds.)

Castellanos' first true dramatic monologue was the "Lamentación de Dido" ("Dido's Lament," from *Poemas*, 1957). In Mexico it is now one of her best loved poems. This long and ambitious work was inspired, as she herself says,[25] by Virgil with regard to content and by St.-Jean Perse with respect to form. She took from the French poet the versicle, the Biblical line or stanza used also by Whitman, and a mythic language and tonality. The story of Dido and Aeneas is from Book IV of the *Aeneid*, but Castellanos also drew on Ovid's *Heroides*.[26] Virgil, and after him Ovid, created the myth of Aeneas and Dido to dramatize the voyage of the Roman hero from Troy to Latium, where, according to the legend, he founded modern Rome. Shipwrecked in Carthage, Aeneas met Queen Dido, who had established that city after a voyage from Phoenicia. The figure of Dido is probably the greatest single literary creation in Roman literature, and it is significant that she was a woman and a member of the defeated nation that was Rome's traditional enemy. Castellanos adapted the details of this legend for the purposes of her poem, from the initial allusions to the murder of Dido's husband by her brother in Phoenicia, to the Mediterranean voyage to the African coast, her meeting with Aeneas, their love and his abandonment of her (urged by the gods in order to fulfill the prophecy of the founding of Rome) and her final self-immolation.

Out of these varied sources Castellanos has forged a powerful statement concerning woman's suffering, abandonment and loneliness; the theme transcends its legendary and pseudo-historical context to become universalized as an expression of woman's subordination to man's activities and selfishness. Dido becomes the timeless symbol of woman oppressed and abandoned:

> And each spring, when the tree gives forth its shoots,
> it is my spirit, not wind without history, my spirit which
>   trembles and makes the foliage sing.
>
> And for my rebirth, year after year,
> I choose from among the many apostrophes that crown me, . . .
> this one, which makes me sister of the sands, forgotten beaches:
> "Dido, she who was abandoned, who placed her heart beneath
>   the blow of a tremendous farewell."

Thus the speaker of the poem, the symbol and legend that was Dido, was chosen by a universal spirit of woman to represent her: between the author and the speaker we discern this universal spirit, who mediates between them and increases the aesthetic distance. Dido describes her princess's education, her ascent to power, the humble skills that were taught by her mother, and the disaster represented by Aeneas who was "cast up by the sea." Throughout the poem we find the motif of woman abandoned:

> —It is woman who remains, a willow branch
> keening on the riverbanks—

So Castellanos' feminist position and ideology finds its avatar in Dido's legend. This legend, and Castellanos' version of it, which stresses the subordination and defeat of woman, can be seen in the context of the historical shift of power from matriarchy to patriarchal society. It is believed that in pre-hellenic and pre-biblical times, the principal gods were female, the *magna mater* of mythology; the Judaic invisible and masculine god supplanted and suppressed the goddess, as society became overwhelmingly patriarchal.[27] Freud, in *Moses and Monotheism*, sees the movement from a sensual god or goddess to an invisible one as "an advance in intellectuality," but Jonathan Culler, in a recent work, suggests that the movement from the visible to the invisible could be a result of the transformation of society from matriarchy (in which biological descent is known, visible) to patriarchy, in which it is invisible (the paternal relation cannot be seen).[28] Astarte was the great goddess of the West Semitic pantheon and the chief deity of Sidon,[29] that is, Phoenicia; and the figure of Dido can be seen as a representative of matriarchal religion. The story of Dido, and Castellanos' version of it in which the point of view is that of woman, may be viewed as an allegory of the displacement of power from the goddess to the god, from Astarte to the Roman Jupiter or Jewish Jehova, and the accompanying transformation of society. Dido, who "remains . . . keening on the riverbank" is an emblem and reminder of that displacement.[30]

The speaker of "Monólogo de la extranjera" ("Monologue of the Foreigner," *Al pie de la letra*, 1959) is a woman who has left one land for another, who feels alienated, a stranger, in her home, and senses the scars of injustice and of slavery in both regions. Like Dido, she is mythicized, larger than life, but she is situated not in classical mythology but in the here and now, in a milieu which appears to be that of Indoamerica, with its racial conflicts and memories of slavery. The poetic speaker survived a difficult childhood in which she slept "beneath the harsh murmur / of a black dove: a defeated race." The reference

is surely to the Mayan Indians of her native Chiapas. She has tasted
fame and power; she has been envied of others, but she feels like a
thorn in the side of her contemporaries, like a dog "barking, in the
midst / of rites and great ceremonies." She seems to have magical pow-
ers, since she ferments "in the thick imagination of others," and her
presence has brought "a saline breath of adventure" to "this somno-
lent inland city."

The speaker of this monologue both is and is not Rosario Castella-
nos. She was not thinking of herself when she wrote it: rather of a
mythical person, almost a shaman, who bears some relation to the
author. "At the moment of writing it," she says,

> . . . I was not conscious of that, I thought that I was
> telling the story of another woman, and on finishing
> it I realized that I was speaking of myself, that it was
> my story, that I had once again transformed it and used
> an oblique form of reference that distances the object
> from the expression . . . perhaps it is aesthetic
> distance.[31]

Referring to this poem and others of *Al pie de la letra*, she wrote that
"I began to recognize my own voice . . . Three threads to follow: hu-
mor, solemn meditation and contact with my carnal and historical
roots."[32] So the mythic figure of Dido, so distant aesthetically from
the author, yet sharing the concern with woman, is transformed, a
few years later, into this "stranger," a native of her own country, with
similar origins and roots, an alter ego. The style is also transformed,
from the metaphoric and mythic mode of "Dido" to humor, simplicity
and meditation: "Youth was serious / but not entirely fatal." The so-
cial concerns and the anger at injustice become more focussed, as her
style evolves toward the colloquialism of "Kinsey Report" and "Self-
Portrait." The poetic speaker of the "Monologue" manages to walk a
thin line between fiction and autobiography, and the reader is never
entirely certain where to situate the poetic voice.

In "Hecuba's Testament," (from *Materia memorable*, 1969), Castellanos
returns to the mythic style of "Dido's Lament," and chooses as speak-
er of her poem the tragic figure from the Greek legends of the Trojan
war. If Dido was the abandoned mistress, Hecuba is the archetypal
maternal figure, strong, dedicated and obedient to masculine authority,
and conscious of her role as bearer and procreator of the race:

So that his name could survive
his body's release
I bore him sons, brave, long-toiling;
virtuous daughters
(except one, a virgin, who kept to herself,
perhaps as an offering to a god.)

When the lightening bolt struck — the Greeks and the war — she accepts defeat, slavery and humiliation with dignity and resignation: "Enslaved queen who never / lost her regal bearing." Like the Mother of Lorca's *Blood Wedding* (also an archetypal figure) Hecuba witnesses and accepts with resigned despair the death of sons and husband; left alone and in misery, she slowly consents "to the consummation, within me, / of the final mysteries." Both in Lorca's play and in Castellanos' poem, the mother is situated at the center of human life and suffering, and it is she, not the heroic masculine figures, who receives the full weight of the tragedy. In contemporary society also it is frequently the woman, mother and widow, who survives to prolong memory and sorrow. Opposed to the archetypal mother is the dispossessed daughter of "Malinche" (from *En la tierra de en medio*, 1972), the Indian princess, both historical and legendary, who was given to Cortés and was instrumental in the conquest of Mexico. Unlike the two previous dramatic monologues dealing with legendary figures of woman, this one does not summarize and universalize the speaker's life, but presents only a moment, the initial one of dispossession, of her story (see notes to the poems).

Although they belong to different collections, both "Kinsey Report" and "Self-Portrait" appeared in the same volume, *Poesía no eres tú* (1972). Both poems are in Castellanos' mature, straightforward, conversational style. "Kinsey Report" is a satirical dramatic monologue in which there are several personae: the married middle-class woman, the unmarried but uninhibited secretary, the divorcée, the *beata* (the prudish dedicated church-goer), the lesbian and the *señorita*. Nearly all strata of Mexican women are covered except, perhaps significantly, the poorest classes, the maids, factory workers and the itinerant Indian women (the *Marias*). Did Castellanos feel too deep a compassion for these women to subject them to her satire? They are, after all, the true sacrificial victims, at the bottom of the economic ladder, unable to better themselves. Each of the personae is weak and has an unsatisfactory sex life, except for the lesbian, who seems content in her relationship but antagonistic toward the rest of society. But each of these women can be interpreted as victims of oppressive sexual and cultural mores: the married woman has been taught since childhood that sex is "indecent" and she only suggests the possibility of orgasm and enjoyment: "No, I don't like it in the least. / Anyway, I shouldn't like it because / I am a decent woman and he's so gross!" The secretary has solved her problem by going out with a variety of men, whom she claims to despise: she is motivated more by fear of loneliness than by desire for sex. We glimpse the beata's imperfect abstinence, her desire that breaks out in dreams. The señorita is perhaps the most pervasively symbolic figure, in this gallery of women in traditional Latin American society: she is woman whose role in life seems to consist in waiting: waiting for a boyfriend, a husband; waiting at home for the return of her working spouse; for the arrival of children. Above all, waiting for Prince Charming, the fairy tale idealizations (Cinderella, Sleeping Beauty, Snow White) of the virgin for whom the arrival of the perfect mate will solve all of her problems. We know when she says "tomorrow" that he will never arrive; she will probably marry and her life will repeat the distresses and dissatisfactions of the first speaker. Society is at fault, but so is the docility of women who accept the dictates of the *nom-du-père*; what is needed is transformation, both of society and of woman's perception of herself, "another way of being, free and human" (from "Meditation on the Threshold").

"Self-Portrait"

This is clearly the most autobiographic of Castellanos' dramatic monologues. There is no detail which does not correspond to the facts of her life; she was married, she had a child (Gabriel); she taught at the University and wrote poems and essays, even to the detail of living across from a park. Between those who maintain that the speaker of a poem is always a fictional creation of the author (M. C. Beardsley, *Aesthetics* and G. T. Wright, *The Poet in the Poem*), and those who, like W. J. Ong (*The Barbarian Within*) insist that a poem is a "cry" directed by a real person to a real reader, there is the middle position taken by Félix Martínez-Bonati, who both avoids and resolves the opposition by suggesting that the reader *becomes* the speaker:

> Similarly, the reader of, or the listener to, lyric poetry
> is able to inhabit unreservedly the poem's expressive
> dimension — that is, possess the words not just in their

representative dimension or solely as imaginary listener, but also, and essentially, *as speaker* (the predominant dimension of lyric poetry) — because of the poem's imaginary existence, because it is not real discourse by the poet.[33]

A successful poem is always relived by the sympathetic reader, who sees the events, feels the emotions, from the point of view of the poem's persona; it is therefore, in the final analysis, irrelevant to concern ourselves with the autonomy of the speaker. Yet, certainly, in this instance, there is apparently a close identification between the speaker and the author; it is Eliot's "first voice of poetry," in which the poet is speaking in her own person — "to himself . . . or addressing a real live audience."[34] In other of her dramatic monologues, like "Valium 10," there is a more conscious creation of a persona, since some of the details do not correspond to her own life. But we shall see that the identification in "Autorretrato" is also illusory.

The first line, with its untranslatable "Señora" ("Yo soy una señora"), is redolent of ironies. Señora (married woman), like Mrs., is a title, but it may be used, as here, as a substantive, and it connotes feelings of power and pride, a station in life, which of course is absent from our more neutral "Mrs." The speaker "shows off her trophy" and adds that it is "more useful / for mingling with others than a degree / from an institution of higher learning." Simone de Beauvoir has described how our various societies place marriage at the pinnacle of a young girl's ambitions:

> Marriage is not only an honorable career and one less tiring than many others: it alone permits a woman to keep her social dignity intact and at the same time to find sexual fulfillment as a loved one and mother . . . There is unanimous agreement that getting a husband . . . is for her the most important of undertakings. In her eyes man incarnates the Other, as she does for man; but this *Other*, and with reference to him, she sees herself as the inessential. She will free herself from the parental home, from her mother's hold, she will open up her future, not by active conquest but by delivering herself up, passive and docile, into the hands of a new master.[35]

Within the patriarchy, the Name-of-the-Father, she is delivered from
one male authority to another; she has little choice, at least in Latin
American society, where the unmarried woman, the non-mother, no
matter how talented, will always remain alienated, unrespected by the
society which has clearly defined woman's role, and does not allow for
deviation. In addition, the phrase "a title difficult / to obtain (in my
case) . . ." suggests the hardships and compromises the speaker had
to accept in order to reach that status. "(In my case)" is an enigmatic
phrase that implies the difficulties that an intellectual and ambitious
woman, in Mexican society, would have in finding an adequate mate.
She says she is "more or less ugly. But that depends / on the hand
that applies the makeup." And "I am mediocre." All this points to the
importance of physical beauty as the prime *desideratum* for a woman
in her culture; the English-speaking reader, who is accustomed to some-
what different mores, to a degree less of attention given to cosmetics,
would need to observe the ubiquitousness of beauty parlors in Mexi-
co and the excesses (in our terms) of make-up used by middle-class
Mexican women. Castellanos, through her speaker, is acutely aware
of the dilemma faced by a creative woman who wants to preserve her
autonomy and authenticity, but at the same time needs to attract the
male and to conform to the expectations of society.[36]

In the following lines, speaking of the men "who send long letters
of congratulations, . . . slowly sip whiskey on the rocks / and talk of
politics and literature," we find another kind of alienation: from the
Other that is for her the impenetrable world of men and their discourse.
But, ironically, it is the very "mediocrity" of her appearance that per-
mits friendships with them, because if her appearance had been more
striking, barriers of a sexual nature would impede the existence of a
relaxed and easy flowing relationship.

Toward the end of the poem she refers to an unattainable happi-
ness; and she ascribes this situation to her education, her insertion
in the symbolic order.

> I would be happy, if I knew how.
> That is, if they had taught me the gestures,
> the speeches, the embellishments.

The speaker (again ironically) abdicates her autonomy and initiative;
it is society's fault, because of the way she (and other young girls) were
brought up for suffering and submission, instead of for masculine pur-
suits and attainments. "Instead they taught me how to weep." Although

she doesn't cry for catastrophes or "sublime occasions," but when the rice is burnt or when she can't find a tax receipt. Castellanos' feminist protest is always ironic and for that reason more effective. Because her role as a woman is carefully prescribed by society, the Name-of-the-Father, the speaker in this poem (who seems to move farther and farther from the author) accepts, but gently laments, her destiny that was defined by the symbolic order. But she has ways of eluding that destiny: although she knows how to weep, she doesn't weep at the right, prescribed times.

"Woman," wrote Simone de Beauvoir, "is shown to us as enticed by two modes of alienation. Evidently, to play at being a man will be for her a source of frustration; but to play at being a woman is also a delusion: to be a woman would mean to be the object, the *Other* — and the Other nevertheless remains subject in the midst of her resignation."[37] These two modes of alienation are at the core of "Self-Portrait." On the one hand, she envies the freedom and *disponibilité* of her male friends; but to play at being a man is useless. On the other hand, if she accepts the role of woman that society has assigned her, and all the inauthenticities and play-acting that go with that role, she becomes an object, the Other, while remaining a subject. The sadness beneath the poem's light tone speaks to us of that resignation and that dilemma.

Although much of her poetry is feminist, in the final analysis her art transcends feminism: throughout there is a concern for all suffering and a seeking for an end to injustice. Her friend José Emilio Pacheco has best summed it up:

> Time and time again the poetry of Rosario Castellanos reminded us that life is not eternal and that suffering is not an accidental annoyance, but rather the condition of life itself. But she did it in a language of such fluidity and luminosity that the final impression does not relate to grief but to the joy before a fully realized work of art.[38]

Notes

[1] The poems quoted only in English translation may be found in the bilingual anthology that follows; those quoted in both Spanish and English are from the volume of Rosario Castellanos' collected poetry, *Poesía no eres tú* (México, D. F.: Fondo de Cultura Económica, 1972), which will hereafter be abbreviated as *PNET*.

[2] In this discussion I will be using some of the terminology that has derived from the work of the French psychoanalyst Jacques Lacan, who has expanded and refined Freud's thought. Lacan's concepts do not comprise a "method" that can be directly applied to literature; they are rather a context, a new perspective, which may change our conceptions of language and the work of art. Here are some of the concepts which I will be alluding to: the child who has not yet learned to speak enters into the *imaginary state*, in which he manages to capture his image in a mirror or in the image of a playmate. He then is gradually incorporated into the *symbolic order*, the world of language and custom, of the signifier. The adolescent and the adult are fully immersed in the symbolic order and are in a sense prisoners of this order, of culture and language. They have suffered a *splitting (Spaltung)* between the unconscious, the *real*, the most truthful part of our being, and the subject of conscious discourse, of culture and social behavior (the ego). The Name-of-the-Father (*nom-du-père*) refers to the male-paternal domination of our historical culture: laws, strictures and prohibitions, and not to any particular or real father. For good expositions of Lacan's thought, see Anthony Wilden, ed., *Jacques Lacan, The Language of the Self* (New York: Delta, 1968), and Anika Lemaire, *Jacques Lacan*, trans. David Macey, (London: Routledge and Kegan Paul, 1977).

[3] Quoted in Maureen Ahern and Mary Seale Vásquez, eds., *Homenaje a Rosario Castellanos* (see end bibliography), from Beth Miller in *Feminist Studies*, 3 (Spring-Summer 1976), 68.

[4] Mary Seale Vásquez, in *Homenaje . . .* , p. 21.

[5] The title is from the Spanish proverb, "Mujer que sabe latín ni tiene marido ni tiene buen fin" ("A woman who knows Latin has neither a husband nor will come to a good end.")

[6] "American feminism seems to be the image of that which it should not be (*de ce qu'il ne faut pas faire*); it has created a true battle of the sexes which appears in film as in literature, or in professional life. One clearly sees the dangers. France has the good fortune of being a country half Celtic, half Latin, and there exists here a tradition of humor among its beings, totally absent in the puritans, who display a distance and social hypocrisy responsible for the present state of affairs. That could not happen in France, where one knows how to laugh at oneself, and happily moreover, because, after all, most women are destined to live with a man!" From an interview with Groult in the *Journal Français d'Amérique*, 5, nos. 14–15, July–August 4, 1983, p. 12.

[7] On the subject of her feminism, see Gabriella de Beer's introduction to this volume and Eliana Rivero's article listed in the bibliography.

[8] Jane Gallop, *The Daughter's Seduction: Feminism and Psychoanalysis* (Ithaca: Cornell Univ. Press, 1982), p. 39.

[9] Gallop, p. 40.

[10] *Les Structures élémentaires de la parenté*, quoted in Simone de Beauvior, *The Second Sex* (New York: Vintage Books, 1974), p. 80.

[11] "Men's feeling that we are not really human originates in their infancy. It resonates, moreover, with the atmosphere of our own infancy: this is what most essentially muffles our shock, dulls our indignation, when we encounter it. Our own reactive feeling—that it is men who are not really human, 'not all there'—comes later and is far less primitive." Dorothy Dinnerstein, *The Mermaid and the Minotaur: Sexual Arrangements and Human Malaise* (New York: Harper and Row, 1976), pp. 91, 93. Dinnerstein believes that it is the exclusively female nurturing of infants that creates these attitudes.

[12] On man's envy of woman, see Karen Horney, "The Flight From Womanhood," in Horney, *Feminine Psychology*, ed. Harold Kelman (New York: W. W. Norton, 1967), pp. 54–70. "Is not the tremendous strength in men of the impulse to creative work in every field precisely due to their feelings of playing a relatively small part in the creation of living beings, which constantly impels them to an overcompensation in achievement?" (p. 61).

[13] What, then, we may ask, is the aim of feminism? Is it to persuade women to try to resemble the predatory and competitive male? Will her participation in business, education and government make her more "masculine," or will it, on the contrary, inject into the affairs of state and commerce a feminine compassion and understanding? Theodor Adorno, reflecting on the ideas of Thorstein Veblen, makes the following comment: "Hope cannot aim at making the mutilated social character of women identical to the mutilated social character of men; rather its goal must be a state in which the face of grieving woman disappears simultaneously with that of the bustling, capable man, a state in which all that survives the disgrace of the difference between the sexes is the happiness that difference makes possible." Adorno, *Prisms*, trans. Samuel and Sherry Weber (Cambridge, Mass.: The MIT Press, 1981), p. 82.

[14] See Juliet Mitchell and Jacqueline Rose, eds., *Feminine Sexuality: Jacques Lacan and the école freudienne* (New York: W. W. Norton, 1982), p. 25 and ff.

[15] See Jacques Lacan, *The Four Fundamental Concepts of Psycho-Analysis*, trans. Alan Sheridan (New York: W. W. Norton, 1981), esp. Chapter 14, "The Partial Drive and Its Circuit," and the definition of desire on p. 278: "It [desire] is not appetite; it is essentially excentric and insatiable. That is why Lacan co-ordinates it not with the object that would seem to satisfy it, but with the object that causes it."

[16] Gallop, p. 35.

[17] Mukarovsky, *The Word and Verbal Art* (New Haven: Yale Univ. Press, 1977), Chapter 2, "Two Studies of Poetic Designation."

[18] Mukarovsky, p. 79.

[19] Mukarovsky, p. 80.

[20] Victor Shklovsky in Lee T. Lemon and Marion J. Reis, eds., *Russian Formalist Criticism* (Lincoln: Univ. of Nebraska Press, 1965), p. 13.

[21] See Andrew Debicki, *Poetry of Discovery* (Lexington: The University Press of Kentucky, 1982), Chapters 3 and 4.

[22] Mary Jacobus, ed., *Women Writing and Writing about Women* (London: Croom Helm, 1979), p. 13.

[23] Jacobus, p. 16.

[24] Alex Preminger, ed. *Princeton Encyclopedia of Poetry and Poetics* (Princeton: Princeton Univ. Press, 1974), p. 529.

[25] *Mujer que sabe latín . . .* , p. 207.

[26] See Ovid's *Heroides*, trans. Harold C. Cannon (New York: E. P. Dutton, 1971), Letter VII, "Dido to Aeneas," pp. 52–58, in which the events of Dido's early life are recounted.

[27] See Erich Neumann, *The Great Mother: An Analysis of the Archetype* (Princeton: Princeton Univ. Press, 1974), and Andrew M. Greely, *The Mary Myth: On the Femininity of God* (New York: Seabury Press, 1977).

[28] See Jonathan Culler, *On Deconstruction: Theory and Criticism after Structuralism* (Ithaca: Cornell Univ. Press, 1982), p. 59.

[29] "Astarte," *New Encyclopedia Britannica: Micropaedia*, 1977.

[30] "On various occasions Rosario Castellanos has said that her poetry is not autobiographical, but speaking of 'Dido's Lament' she confessed that with this poem she wished to 'salvage an experience . . . through an image situated in the timeless, in tradition.' " Gabriella de Beer, "Feminismo en la obra poética de Rosario Castellanos," p. 107. The quotation is from Emanuel Carballo, *Diecinueve protagonistas de la literatura mexicana*, p. 416.

[31] From an interview with Margarita García Flores, "La lucidez como forma de vida," *La onda*, supplement to *Novedades* (Mexico City), Aug. 18, 1974. Quoted in Ahern and Seale Vásquez, *Homenaje a Rosario Castellanos*, p. 28.

[32] *Mujer que sabe latín . . .*, p. 207.

[33] Félix Martínez-Bonati, *Fictive Discourse and the Structures of Literature*, trans. Philip W. Silver (Ithaca: Cornell Univ. Press, 1981), p. 96. Italics mine.

[34] Preminger, p. 960.

[35] De Beauvior, *The Second Sex*, p. 368.

[36] With regard to the question of her appearance, the reference to Weininger in the fifth strophe requires some explanation. Weininger, a turn-of-the-century German writer on sex and psychology, created a brief flurry with his ideas on feminine inferiority and the distribution of sexual characteristics among males and females. He believed that the appearance of persons of genius undergoes "almost incredible changes" from time to time, and he mentions portraits of Goethe, Beethoven, Kant and Schopenhauer to prove his point. "The number of different aspects that the face of man has assumed may be taken almost as a physiognomical measure of his talent." (Otto Weininger, *Sex and Character*; London: William Heinemann, 1912, p. 108). Just why Castellanos chose to allude to a discredited, forgotten and racist (anti-Semitic) writer is curious; perhaps he represented for her the ultimate in male sexism, and from her feminist point of view he needed to be denounced, if only by this ironic gesture.

[37] *The Second Sex*, p. 52.

[38] José Emilio Pacheco, Prologue to Castellano's *El uso de la palabra*, p. 13.

A Bilingual Anthology

from

Poesía no eres tú

1950–1972

Meditación en el umbral

No, no es la solución
tirarse bajo un tren como la Ana de Tolstoi
ni apurar el arsénico de Madame Bovary
ni aguardar en los páramos de Avila la visita
del ángel con venablo
antes de liarse el manto a la cabeza
y comenzar a actuar.

Ni concluir las leyes geométricas, contando
las vigas de la celda de castigo
como lo hizo Sor Juana. No es la solución
escribir, mientras llegan las visitas,
en la sala de estar de la familia Austen
ni encerrarse en el ático
de alguna residencia de la Nueva Inglaterra
y soñar, con la Biblia de los Dickinson,
debajo de una almohada de soltera.

Debe haber otro modo que no se llame Safo
ni Mesalina ni María Egipciaca
ni Magdalena ni Clemencia Isaura.[1]

Otro modo de ser humano y libre.

Otro modo de ser.

Meditation on the Threshold

No, it's no solution
to throw yourself under the wheels of a train
like Tolstoy's Anna
nor to down the poisoned cup of Madame Bovary
nor to wait on the high plains of Avila
for the visit of an angel armed with a javelin
before tying your robe around your head
and starting to act.

Nor to review the laws of geometry
while counting the beams of your punishment cell
like Sor Juana Inés. Nor is the solution
to write in the Austen living room
while the guests are arriving,
nor to close yourself up in an attic
of a New England home
and to dream with the Dickinson family Bible
beneath your virgin's pillow.

There must be some other way that is not
called Sappho or Messalina or Mary
of Egypt or Magdalena or Clemencia Isaura.[1]

Another way of being, free and human.

Another manner of being.

Otros poemas

Origen

Sobre el cadáver de una mujer estoy creciendo,
en sus huesos se enroscan mis raíces
y de su corazón desfigurado
emerge un tallo vertical y duro.
Del féretro de un niño no nacido:
de su vientre tronchado antes de la cosecha
me levanto tenaz, definitiva,
brutal como una lápida y en ocasiones triste
con la tristeza pétrea del ángel funerario
que oculta entre sus manos una cara sin lágrimas.

Origin

Over the dead body of a woman I am growing,
on her bones my roots are coiled
and from her disfigured heart
emerges a hard, vertical stalk.
From the coffin of an unborn child:
from its stomach shattered before the harvest
I rise up, tenacious, definitive,
brutal as a gravestone and on occasion sad
with the stony weariness of a funeral angel
who hides a tearless visage beneath his hands.

De la vigilia estéril

Silencio cerca de una piedra antigua

Estoy aquí, sentada, con todas mis palabras
como una cesta de fruta verde, intactas.

Los fragmentos
de mil dioses antiguos derribados
se buscan por mi sangre, se aprisionan, queriendo
recomponer su estatua.
De las bocas destruidas
quiere subir hasta mi boca un canto,
un olor de resinas quemadas, algún gesto
de misteriosa roca trabajada.
Pero soy el olvido, la traición,
el caracol que no guardó del mar
ni el eco de la más pequeña ola.
Y no miro los templos sumergidos;
sólo miro los árboles que encima de las ruinas
mueven su vasta sombra, muerden con dientes ácidos
el viento cuando pasa.
Y los signos se cierran bajo mis ojos como
la flor bajo los dedos torpísimos de un ciego.
Pero yo sé: detrás
de mi cuerpo otro cuerpo se agazapa,
y alrededor de mí muchas respiraciones
cruzan furtivamente
como los animales nocturnos en la selva.
Yo sé, en algún lugar,
lo mismo
que en el desierto el cactus,
un constelado corazón de espinas
está aguardando un nombre como el cactus la lluvia.
Pero yo no conozco más que ciertas palabras
en el idioma o lápida
bajo el que sepultaron vivo a mi antepasado.

Silence Near an Ancient Stone

I sit here with all my words, words that
are impaired, intact like a basket of ripe fruit.

The fragments
of a thousand demolished ancient gods
seek themselves in my blood, imprisoned,
attempting to restore their statue.
From their ruined mouths
a song tries to rise to my lips,
an odor of burnt resin, a gesture
of mysterious sculpted stone.
But I am forgetfulness, betrayal,
the seashell that has not retained an echo
of the slightest wave.
And I don't see the submerged temples;
I see only the trees that move their vast shadows
over the ruins, the trees that bite with acidic teeth
the wind as it passes.
And the signs crumble beneath my eyes
like a flower under the clumsy fingers of a blind man.
But I know: underneath
my body another body crouches,
and breaths cross furtively around me
like nocturnal animals in the jungle.
I know in some place
like
a cactus in the desert,
a spray, a heart of thorns
is abiding my name as a cactus
waits for rain.
But I only know certain words
in the language or gravestone beneath which
they buried my ancestor alive.

El rescate del mundo

Lavanderas de Grijalva

Pañuelo del adiós,
camisa de la boda,
en el río, entre peces
jugando con las olas.

Como un recién nacido
bautizado, esta ropa
ostenta su blancura
total y milagrosa.

Mujeres de la espuma
y el ademán que limpia,
halladme un río hermoso
para lavar mis días.

Washerwomen of Grijalva

Wedding-day blouse,
kerchief of farewell,
in the river, among fish
playing with the swell.

Like a newborn, just-
baptized child,
these clothes show a total
miraculous white.

Women of the foam
and the gesture that laves,
find me a lovely river
to cleanse my days.

El rescate del mundo

A la mujer que vende frutas en la plaza

Amanece en las jícaras
y el aire que las toca se esparce como ebrio.
Tendrías que cantar para decir el nombre
de estas frutas, mejores que tus pechos.

Con reposo de hamaca
tu cintura camina
y llevas a sentarse entre las otras
una ignorante dignidad de isla.

Me quedaré a tu lado,
amiga,
hablando con la tierra
todo el día.

To the Fruit Vendor in the Plaza

The sun rises on your gourds
and the air they touch scatters like a drunk.
Only singing could you say the name
of those fruits, that outshine your breasts.

With a hammock's repose
your waist glides
and you sit among the others
with a simple dignity of islands.

I shall remain by your side,
my friend,
all the livelong day
conversing with the earth.

El rescate del mundo

La oración del indio

El indio sube al templo tambaleándose,
ebrio de sus sollozos como de un alcohol fuerte.
Se para frente a Dios a exprimir su miseria
y grita con un grito de animal acosado
y golpea entre sus puños su cabeza.

El borbotón de sangre que sale por su boca
deja su cuerpo quieto.

Se tiende, se abandona, duerme en el mismo suelo
que la juncia y respira
el aire de la cera y del incienso.

Repose largamente
tu inocencia de manos que no crucificaron.
Repose tu confianza
reclinada en el brazo del Amor
como un pequeño pueblo en una cordillera.

Indian's Prayer

The Indian stumbles up the church steps
drunk from his sobbing as from a strong liquor.
He stands before his God to give forth his wretchedness
and cries out like a cornered animal
and beats his fists against his temples.

Out of his mouth slips a froth of blood
that leaves his body still.

Exhausted, he stretches out, sleeps
on the sedge-strewn floor
and breathes the air of wax and incense.

May your innocence of hands
that did not crucify   ˋ
find a lasting rest.
May your faith repose
fast in the arms of Love
like a small village in a mountain range.

El rescate del mundo

Lamentación de Dido[2]

Guardiana de las tumbas; botín para mi hermano, el de la
        corva garra de gavilán;
nave de airosas velas, nave graciosa, sacrificada al rayo de
        las tempestades;
mujer que asienta por primera vez la planta del pie en
        tierras desoladas
y es más tarde nodriza de naciones, nodriza que amamanta
        con leche de sabiduría y de consejo;
mujer siempre, y hasta el fin, que con el mismo pie de la
        sagrada peregrinación
sube —arrastrando la oscura cauda de su memoria— hasta la
        pira alzada del suicidio.

Tal es el relato de mis hechos. Dido mi nombre. Destinos
como el mío se han pronunciado desde la antigüedad con
        palabras hermosas y nobilísimas.
Mi cifra se grabó en la corteza del árbol enorme de las
        tradiciones
Y cada primavera, cuando el árbol retoña,
es mi espíritu, no el viento sin historia, es mi espíritu el
        que estremece y el que hace cantar su follaje.

Y para renacer, año con año,
escojo entre los apóstrofes que me coronan, para que
        resplandezca con un resplandor único,
éste, que me da cierto parentesco con las playas:
Dido, la abandonada, la que puso su corazón bajo el
        hachazo de un adiós tremendo.

Yo era lo que fui: mujer de investidura desproporcionada
        con la flaqueza de su ánimo.
Y, sentada a la sombra de un solio inmerecido,
temblé bajo la púrpura igual que el agua tiembla bajo el
        légamo.

Dido's Lament[2]

Guardian of tombs; booty for my brother, he of the curved
        hawk's claw,
graceful ship of proud sails, sacrificed to the storm's fury;
woman who sets foot for the first time on a desolate land;
later wet nurse of nations, offering the milk of her wisdom;
woman always, to the end, who with steps of sacred
        pilgrimage
ascends — dragging the dark weight of her memory —
the high suicide's pyre.

Such is the tale of my deeds. Dido my name. Destinies
like mine have been sung since antiquity with splendid,
        lovely words.
My device was carved in the bark of the enormous tree of
        traditions.
And each spring, when the tree gives forth its shoots,
it is my spirit, not wind without history, my spirit which
        trembles and makes the foliage sing.

And for my rebirth, year after year,
I choose from among the many apostrophes that crown me,
        so that it may shine with unmatched splendor
this one, which makes me sister of the sands, forgotten
        beaches:
"Dido, she who was abandoned, who placed her heart
        beneath the blow of a tremendous farewell."

I was a woman invested with authority out of proportion to
        my spirit's strength.
And seated in the shade of an unmerited throne,
I trembled under the purple as water trembles beneath the
        slime.

Y para obedecer mandatos cuya incomprensibilidad me
        sobrepasa recorrí las baldosas de los pórticos
        con la balanza de la justicia entre mis manos
y pesé las acciones y declaré mi consentimiento para
        algunas—las más graves.

Esto era en el día. Durante la noche no la copa del festín,
        no la alegría de la serenata, no el sueño
        deleitoso.
Sino los ojos acechando en la oscuridad, la inteligencia
        batiendo la selva intrincada de los textos
para cobrar la presa que huye entre las páginas.
Y mis oídos, habituados a la ardua polémica de los
        mentores,
llegaron a ser hábiles para distinguir el robusto sonido del
        oro
del estrépito estéril con que entrechocan los guijarros.

De mi madre, que no desdeñó mis manos y que me las
        ungió desde el amanecer con la destreza,
heredé oficios varios; cardadora de lana, escogedora del
        fruto que ilustra la estación y su clima,
despabiladora de lámparas.

Así pues tomé la rienda de mis días: potros domados,
        conocedores del camino, reconocedores de la
        querencia.
Así pues ocupé mi sitio en la asamblea de los mayores.
Y a la hora de la partición comí apaciblemente el pan que
        habían amasado mis deudos.
Y con frecuencia sentí deshacerse entre mi boca el grano de
        sal de un acontecimiento dichoso.

Pero no dilapidé mi lealtad. La atesoraba para el tiempo de
        las lamentaciones,
para cuando los cuervos aletean encima de los tejados y
        mancillan la transparencia del cielo con su
        graznido fúnebre;

And in order to obey dimly understood commands, I
        traversed the tiled porticos, the scale of justice
        in my hands;
I weighed the actions and declared my consent for some of
        the gravest.

That was by day. By night there was neither festive cup,
        nor music's joy, nor the release of sleep,
but eyes lurking in the darkness, intelligence beating the
        confused jungle of texts
to capture the prey that flees among pages.
And my ears, accustomed to the harsh polemics of mentors,
became skillful in distinguishing the robust sound of gold
from the sterile clatter of pebbles.

From my mother (who not disdaining my hands, anointed
        them from early dawn with many skills),
I inherited various dexterities: carder of wool; she who
        selected the season's and climate's most
        succulent fruit;
lamptrimmer.

Thus I held tightly to the leash of my days: tame colts,
        familiar with the road, responsive to desire.
And I took my place in the assembly of the elders;
at the hour of repartition, I ate peacefully the bread whose
        dough my kinsmen had kneaded.
And frequently I let dissolve in my mouth the salt grain of
        a joyful event.

But I did not squander my loyalty. I cherished it for the
        time of lamentations,
for that time when the crows wheel above rooftops and stain
        the sky's clarity with the cawing;

para cuando la desgracia entra por la puerta principal de las
        mansiones
y se la recibe con el mismo respeto que a una reina.

De este modo transcurrió mi mocedad: en el cumplimiento
        de las menudas tareas domésticas; en la
        celebración de los ritos cotidianos; en la
        asistencia a los solemnes acontecimientos
        civiles.

Y yo dormía, reclinando mi cabeza sobre una almohada de
        confianza.
Así la llanura, dilatándose, puede creer en la benevolencia
        de su sino,
porque ignora que la extensión no es más que la pista
        donde corre, como un atleta vencedor,
enrojecido por el heroísmo supremo de su esfuerzo, la llama
        del incendio.
Y el incendio vino a mí, la predación, la ruina, el
        exterminio
¡y no he dicho el amor!, en figura de náufrago.

Esto que el mar rechaza, dije, es mío.
Y ante él me adorné de la misericordia como del brazalete
        de más precio.
Yo te conjuro, si oyes, a que respondas: ¿quién esquivó la
        adversidad alguna vez? ¿Y quién tuvo a
        desdoro llamarle huésped suya y preparar la
        sala del convite?
Quien lo hizo no es mi igual. Mi lenguaje se entronca con
        el de los inmoladores de sí mismos.

El cuchillo bajo el que se quebró mi cerviz era un hombre
        llamado Eneas.
Aquel Eneas, aquel, piadoso con los suyos solamente;
acogido a la fortaleza de muros extranjeros; astuto, con
        astucias de bestia perseguida;

when misfortune enters the principal gate of the mansions
and it is received with the same respect accorded a queen.

My youth passed in this fashion: in the fulfillment of small
      domestic tasks; in the celebration of daily
      rituals; attending the solemn civil functions.

And I slept, reclining my head on a familiar pillow,
just as the plain, when it unfolds, may believe in the
      benevolence of its fate
because it is unaware that its expanse is merely the track on
      which runs the flame of a devastating blaze,
like a victorious athlete, flushed by his supreme, heroic
      effort.
And that fire drew near me with plunder, ruin,
      extermination
—I haven't said love!—in the form of a man cast up by the
      sea.

I said: that which the sea rejects is mine.
And before him I clothed myself in pity, as with a most
      precious jewel.
And I entreat you (if you hear) to respond: who has ever
      turned away from adversity? Who thought it
      sullying to call it a guest, to prepare the
      reception hall?
Whoever refused such is not my equal. I speak the language
      of those who perish in self-immolation.

The knife which severed my neck was a man called Aeneas.
Aeneas, who was merciful only with his own kind;
drawn to the strength of foreign walls; astute like a hunted
      wild animal;

invocador de númenes favorables; hermoso narrador de
    infortunios y hombre de paso; hombre
con el corazón puesto en el futuro.

  —La mujer es la que permanece; rama de sauce que llora
    en las orillas de los ríos—.

Y yo amé a aquel Eneas, a aquel hombre de promesa
    jurada ante otros dioses.

Lo amé con mi ceguera de raíz, con mi soterramiento de
    raíz, con mi lenta fidelidad de raíz.

No, no era la juventud. Era su mirada lo que así me cubría
    de florecimientos repentinos. Entonces yo fui
    capaz de poner la palma de mi mano, en signo
    de alianza, sobre la frente de la tierra. Y vi
    acercarse a mí, amistades, las especies hostiles.
    Y vi también reducirse a número los astros. Y
    oí que el mundo tocaba su flauta de pastor.

Pero esto no era suficiente. Y yo cubrí mi rostro con la
    máscara nocturna del amante.
Ah, los que aman apuran tósigos mortales. Y el veneno
    enardeciendo su sangre, nublando sus ojos,
    trastornando su juicio, los conduce a cometer
    actos desatentados; a menospreciar aquello que
    tuvieron en más estima; a hacer escarnio de su
    túnica y a arrojar su fama como pasto para que
    hocen los cerdos.
Así, aconsejada de mis enemigos, di pábulo al deseo y
    maquiné satisfacciones ilícitas y tejí un espeso
    manto de hipocresía para cubrirlas.

Pero nada permanece oculto a la venganza. La tempestad
    presidió nuestro ayuntamiento; la reprobación
    fue el eco de nuestras decisiones.

he who invoked the favor of gods; wayfarer, splendid
        narrator of misfortunes; a man
with his heart anchored in the future.

—It is woman who remains, a willow branch keening on
        the riverbanks—.

And I loved Aeneas, that man already beholden to other
        gods.

I loved him with the blindness of a buried root, with a slow
        root-like tenacity and fidelity.

No, it was not my youth, but his glance that covered me
        with a sudden flowering. Then I was capable of
        placing the palm of my hand, as a sign of
        alliance, on the earth's forehead. And I
        witnessed the approach of friends, of hostile
        species. And I saw the stars diminish. I heard
        the world play its shepherd flute.

But this was not enough. I covered my face with the
        nocturnal mask of my beloved.
Ah, those who love drink a mortal venom. Inflaming the
        blood, it blinds their eyes, warps their reason;
        makes them perform senseless actions; scorn
        those whom they most esteemed; ridicule their
        tunics and cast away their fame like fodder for
        the snout of swine.
Thus, encouraged by my enemies, I fed my desire, devised
        illicit joys, and wove a thick veil of hypocrisy
        to cover them.

But nothing remains long hidden to vengeance. A storm
        presided over our union; vituperation echoed
        our decisions.

Mirad, aquí y allá, esparcidos, los instrumentos de la labor.
Mirad el ceño del deber defraudado. Porque la
molicie nos había reblandecido los tuétanos.
Y convertida en antorcha yo no supe iluminar más que el
desastre.

Pero el hombre está sujeto durante un plazo menor a la
embriaguez.
Lúcido nuevamente, apenas salpicado por la sangre de la
víctima,
Eneas partió.

Nada detiene al viento. ¡Cómo iba a detenerlo la rama de
sauce que llora en las orillas de los ríos!

En vano, en vano fue correr, destrenzada y frenética, sobre
las arenas humeantes de la playa.

Rasgué mi corazón y echó a volar una bandada de palomas
negras. Y hasta el anochecer permanecí,
incólume como un acantilado, bajo el brutal
abalanzamiento de las olas.

He aquí que al volver ya no me reconozco. Llego a mi casa
y la encuentro arrasada por las furias. Ando
por los caminos sin más vestidura para
cubrirme que el velo arrebatado a la
vergüenza; sin otro cíngulo que el de la
desesperación para apretar mis sienes. Y,
monótona zumbadora, la demencia me persigue
con su aguijón de tábano.

Mis amigos me miran al través de sus lágrimas; mis deudos
vuelven el rostro hacia otra parte. Porque la
desgracia es espectáculo que algunos no deben
contemplar.

Observe, here and there, the scattered instruments of labor.
    Look at the frown of duty despised. Because
    love's joys had softened our marrow.
And, like a torch transfigured, I could illuminate only my
    disaster.

But man's intoxication is briefer than ours.
With newly won lucidity, hardly stained by the blood of his
    victim,
Aeneas departed.

Nothing can stop the wind. Least of all a branch of willow
    that weeps on the riverbank!

In vain, in vain I ran wildly, disheveled, on the steaming
    sand.

I tore at my heart, out of it black doves flew in droves.
    Until nightfall I remained motionless as a rock
    under the brutal pounding of the waves.

Observe: on returning home I no longer recognize myself. I
    find my house razed by the furies. I walk along
    roads covered only by a veil torn from shame;
    with only a band of despair circling my
    temples. And madness, a monotonous buzzing
    about me, pursues with the sting of a gadfly.

My friends watch through the veil of their tears; my
    kinsmen turn away their faces. Because
    misfortune is not a spectacle for all to
    contemplate.

Ah, sería preferible morir. Pero yo sé que para mí no hay
   muerte.
Porque el dolor—¿y qué otra cosa soy más que dolor?—me
   ha hecho eterna.

To die would be the better course. But I know that for me
       there will be no death.
Because grief (and what other name is left for me?) has
       made me eternal.

Poemas

El otro

¿Por qué decir nombres de dioses, astros,
espumas de un océano invisible,
polen de los jardines más remotos?
Si nos duele la vida, si cada día llega
desgarrando la entraña, si cada noche cae
convulsa, asesinada.
Si nos duele el dolor en alguien, en un hombre
al que no conocemos, pero está
presente a todas horas y es la víctima
y el enemigo y el amor y todo
lo que nos falta para ser enteros.
Nunca digas que es tuya la tiniebla,
no te bebas de un sorbo la alegría.
Mira a tu alrededor: hay otro, siempre hay otro.
Lo que él respira es lo que a ti te asfixia,
lo que come es tu hambre.
Muere con la mitad más pura de tu muerte.

The Other

Why pronounce the names of gods, stars,
froth of an invisible ocean,
pollen from the most distant gardens?
If life aches us, if each day comes
tearing us apart, if each night
falls convulsed, assassinated.
If the grief of an unknown person
grieves us, but he is
always present, and is the victim
and the enemy and love and all
that we need in order to be whole.
Never say that the darkness is yours,
don't drink joy down with a single swallow.
Look about you: there is the other, there is always
                  the other.
The air he breathes chokes you,
what he eats is your hunger.
He dies with the purest half of your death.

Al pie de la letra

Dos meditaciones

I

Considera, alma mía, esta textura
áspera al tacto, a la que llaman vida.
Repara en tantos hilos tan sabiamente unidos
y en el color, sombrío pero noble,
firme, y donde ha esparcido su resplandor el rojo.

Piensa en la tejedora; en su paciencia
para recomenzar
una tarea siempre inacabada.

Y odia después, si puedes.

II

Hombrecito, ¿qué quieres hacer con tu cabeza?
¿Atar al mundo, al loco, loco y furioso mundo?
¿Castrar al potro Dios?

Pero Dios rompe el freno y continúa engendrando
magníficas criaturas,
seres salvajes cuyos alaridos
rompen esta campana de cristal.

Two Meditations

I

Consider, my soul, this texture
harsh to the touch, which is called life.
Notice so many threads wisely joined
together, and the color, dark, noble, firm
where red has suffused its splendor.

Think then about the Weaver: her patience
in starting again an always
unfinished task.

And hate, afterwards, if you can.

II

Little man, what would you do with your reason?
Bind up the world, the mad and furious world?
Castrate the colt called God?

But God breaks out of his tethers
and keeps engendering magnificent creatures,
wild beings whose shrieks
shatter this bell jar.

Al pie de la letra

Monólogo de la extranjera

Vine de lejos. Olvidé mi patria.
Ya no entiendo el idioma
que allá usan de moneda o de herramienta.
Alcancé la mudez mineral de la estatua.
Pues la pereza y el desprecio y algo
que no sé discernir me han defendido
de este lenguaje, de este terciopelo
pesado, recamado de joyas, con que el pueblo
donde vivo, recubre sus harapos.

Esta tierra, lo mismo que la otra de mi infancia,
tiene aún en su rostro,
marcada a fuego y a injusticia y crimen,
su cicatriz de esclava.
Ay, de niña dormía bajo el arrullo ronco
de una paloma negra: una raza vencida.
Me escondía entre las sábanas
porque un gran animal
acechaba en la sombra, hambriento, y sin embargo
con la paciencia dura de la piedra.
Junto a él ¿qué es el mar o la desgracia
o el rayo del amor
o la alegría que nos aniquila?

Quiero decir, entonces,
que me fue necesario crecer pronto
(antes de que el terror me devorase)
y partir y poner la mano firme
sobre el timón y gobernar la vida.

Demasiado temprano
escupí en los lugares
que la plebe consagra para la reverencia.
Y entre la multitud yo era como el perro

Monologue of a Foreign Woman

I came from far away. I forgot my country.
I no longer understand the language
used there for money or tools.
I achieved the granite dumbness of a statue.
Laziness and scorn and something
I cannot name have defended me
against this language, of heavy velvet
embroidered with jewels, with which the country and people
where I live cover their rags.

This land, like that other one of my childhood,
still bears on its face,
branded with fire, injustice and crime,
its slave's scar.
When a child I slept beneath the harsh murmur
of a black dove: a defeated race.
I hid beneath the sheets
because a huge animal
was waiting in the shadows, hungry but
with the hard patience of stone.
Compared with it, what is the sea or misfortune
or stroke of love
or happiness which undermines us?

I mean, then,
that I had to grow up quickly
(Before that terror would devour me)
and leave and place a firm hand
on the helm and govern my life.

Too early
did I spit on the places
that the common people consecrate.
And among the multitude I was like a dog

que ofende con su sarna y su fornicación
y su ladrido inoportuno, en medio
del rito y la importante ceremonia.

Y bien. La juventud,
aunque grave, no fue mortal del todo.
Convalecí. Sané. Con pulso hábil
aprendí a sopesar el éxito, el prestigio,
el honor, la riqueza.
Tuve lo que el mediocre envidia, lo que los
triunfadores disputan y uno solo arrebata.
Lo tuve y fue como comer espuma,
como pasar la mano sobre el lomo del viento.

El orgullo supremo es la suprema
renunciación. No quise
ser el astro difunto
que absorbe luz prestada para vivificarse.
Sin nombre, sin recuerdos,
con una desnudez espectral, giro
en una breve órbita doméstica.

Pero aun así fermento
en la imaginación espesa de los otros.
Mi presencia ha traído
hasta esta soñolienta ciudad de tierra adentro
un aliento salino de aventura.

Mirándome, los hombres recuerdan que el destino
es el gran huracán que parte ramas
y abate firmes árboles
y establece en su imperio
—sobre la mezquindad de lo humano—la ley
despiadada del cosmos.

Me olfatean desde lejos las mujeres y sueñan
lo que las bestias de labor, si huelen

that offends with its mange and fornication
and untimely barking, in the midst
of rites and great ceremonies.

Well then. Youth was serious
but not entirely fatal.
I recovered. Got better. With expert pulse
I began to weigh success, prestige,
honor, wealth.
I had what the mediocre envy, what
victors dispute and one alone snatches away.
I had it and it was like eating foam,
like passing one's hand over the back of the wind.

Supreme pride is supreme
renunciation. I didn't want
to be the dead star
that uses borrowed light to survive.
Nameless, without memory,
with a ghostly nakedness, I turn
in a small domestic orbit.

But even so I ferment
in the thick imagination of others.
My presence has brought
even to this somnolent inland city
a saline breath of adventure.

Looking at me, men remember that destiny
is a great hurricane that smashes branches
and knocks down proud trees
and established in its dominion
— over man's baseness —
the merciless law of the cosmos.

Women sniff at me from afar and dream
what work animals dream, when they smell

la ráfaga brutal de la tormenta.
Cumplo también, delante del anciano,
un oficio pasivo:
el de suscitadora de leyendas.

Y cuando, a medianoche,
abro de par en par las ventanas, es para
que el desvelado, el que medita a muerte,
y el que padece el lecho de sus remordimientos
y hasta el adolescente
(bajo de cuya sien arde la almohada)
interroguen lo oscuro en mi persona.

Basta. He callado más de lo que he dicho.
Tostó mi mano el sol de las alturas
y en el dedo que dicen aquí "del corazón"
tengo un anillo de oro con un sello grabado.

El anillo que sirve
para identificar a los cadáveres.

the storm's brutal gusts.
I also fulfill a passive role
before the old:
the reviver of legends.

And when, at midnight,
I throw the windows wide open, it is
so that the insomniac, he that meditates on death,
and he that suffers the bed of remorse
and even the adolescent
(whose pillow burns beneath his head)
may question the darkness within my person.

Enough. I have left unsaid more than I have spoken.
I burned my hand in the highland sun
and on the middle finger — that of the heart —
I wear a gold ring with an engraved seal.

A ring that is useful
for identifying cadavers.

Al pie de la letra

Linaje

Hay cierta raza de hombres
(ahora ya conozco a mis hermanos)
que llevan en el pecho como un agua desnuda
temblando.
Que tienen manos torpes
y todo se les quiebra entre las manos;
que no quieren mirar para no herir
y levantan sus actos
como una estatua de ángel amoroso
y repentinamente degollado.

Raza de la ternura funesta, de Abel
resucitado.

Lineage

There's a certain race of men
(now I know my brothers and sisters)
who harbor in their breast a bit of trembling,
naked water.
Their hands are clumsy,
things break at their touch;
they prefer not to look
in order not to hurt
and they perform their public rites
like a sculpted, enamored angel
that is suddenly beheaded.

Race of ill-omened tenderness, of Abel
returned to life.

Al pie de la letra

La velada del sapo

Sentadito en la sombra
—solemne con tu bocio exoftálmico; cruel
(en apariencia, al menos, debido a la hinchazón
de los párpados); frío,
frío de repulsiva sangre fría.

Sentadito en la sombra miras arder la lámpara.

En torno de la luz hablamos y quizá
uno dice tu nombre.

(Es septiembre. Ha llovido.)

Como por el resorte de la sorpresa, saltas
y aquí estás ya, en medio de la conversación,
en el centro del grito.

¡Con qué miedo sentimos palpitar
el corazón desnudo
de la noche en el campo!

Toad's Nocturne

Seated in the shadows
— how solemn with your exophthalmic goiter; cruel
(in appearance, at least, with your
swollen eyelids); cold,
cold with repulsive cold blood.

Curled up in the shadows you watch our lamp burn.

Around the lantern we talk, someone
perhaps says your name.

(September. It has rained.)

Sprung as if by surprise
you leap and here you are in the midst
of our conversation, in
the center of our screams.

Fear takes hold of us as we sense
the naked heartbeat
of the darkened countryside!

Al pie de la letra

Aporía del bailarín

A Rodolfo Reyes Cortés

Agilísimo héroe:
tu cerviz no conoce este yugo de buey
con que la gravedad unce a los cuerpos.
En ti, exento, nacen,
surgen alas posibles.

Narciso adolescente.
La juventud se ha derramado en ti
cual generoso aceite
y te unge los muslos
y abrillanta el volumen de tu torso.

¿Qué buscas más allá
del movimiento puro y calculado,
del frenesí que agita el tirso de los números?
¿Qué convulsión orgiástica se enmascara en el orden?

Velocidad y ritmo
son deleitoso tránsito y no anhelado término.
Elevas la actitud,
el gesto, el ademán,
hasta el más alto punto de la congelación.

Y la danza se cumple en el reposo.

Pues el oculto nombre
de la deidad que sirves, oh bailarín, es éste:
voluntad estatuaria.

Aporia of the Dancer

To Rodolfo Reyes Cortés

Agilest hero:
your neck doesn't know the ox's yoke
with which gravity subjects our bodies.
From your disengaged spirit
surge possible wings.

Adolescent Narcissus.
Youth flows into you
like a generous oil
it anoints your thighs
and polishes your torso's volume.

What do you seek
beyond pure, calculated movement,
frenzy impelled by the Bacchic staff of numbers?
What orgiastic convulsion lies masked behind order?

Speed and rhythm
are joyful transitions, not desired end.
You exalt gestures, attitudes
to the point of frozen stillness.

And the dance is completed in repose.

The secret name
of the goddess you serve (O dancer) is this:
a passion for
sculpted quiescence.

Al pie de la letra

Agonía fuera del muro

Miro las herramientas,
el mundo que los hombres hacen, donde se afanan,
sudan, paren, cohabitan.

El cuerpo de los hombres, prensado por los días,
su noche de ronquido y de zarpazo
y las encrucijadas en que se reconocen.

Hay ceguera y el hambre los alumbra
y la necesidad, más dura que metales.

Sin orgullo (¿qué es el orgullo? ¿Una vértebra
que todavía la especie no produce?)
los hombres roban, mienten,
como animal de presa olfatean, devoran
y disputan a otro la carroña.

Y cuando bailan, cuando se deslizan
o cuando burlan una ley o cuando
se envilecen, sonríen,
entornan levemente los párpados, contemplan
el vacío que se abre en sus entrañas
y se entregan a un éxtasis vegetal, inhumano.

Yo soy de alguna orilla, de otra parte,
soy de los que no saben ni arrebatar ni dar,
gente a quien compartir es imposible.

No te acerques a mí, hombre que haces el mundo,
déjame, no es preciso que me mates.
Yo soy de los que mueren solos, de los que mueren
de algo peor que vergüenza.

Yo muero de mirarte y no entender.

Agony From Without the Walls

I look at the tools,
the world that men make, where they struggle,
sweat, give birth, cohabitate.

The body of men, compressed by days,
their night of snoring and blows
and the crossings in which they discover each other.

There is blindness and hunger illuminates them
and need, harder than metal.

Without pride (what is pride? A vertebra
the species has not formed yet?)
men steal, lie,
like predatory animals they sniff, they devour
and dispute the carrion with others.

And when they dance, when they slip back
or when they break a law or when
they debase themselves, they smile,
they faintly half-close their eyes, and contemplate
the emptiness that yawns in their breast
and surrender to a vegetal, inhuman ecstasy.

I am from some far shore, from another region,
I am one of those who doesn't know how to grab or how to give,
for whom sharing is impossible.

Don't come near me, man who forges the world,
let me be, you don't need to kill me.
I am one of those who die by themselves, those who die
of something worse than shame.

I die because I look at you and don't understand.

Lívida luz

Jornada de la soltera

Da vergüenza estar sola. El día entero
arde un rubor terrible en su mejilla.
(Pero la otra mejilla está eclipsada.)

La soltera se afana en quehacer de ceniza,
en labores sin mérito y sin fruto;
y a la hora en que los deudos se congregan
alrededor del fuego, del relato,
se escucha el alarido
de una mujer que grita en un páramo inmenso
en el que cada peña, cada tronco
carcomido de incendios, cada rama
retorcida, es un juez
o es un testigo sin misericordia.

De noche la soltera
se tiende sobre el lecho de agonía.
Brota un sudor de angustia a humedecer las sábanas
y el vacío se puebla
de diálogos y hombres inventados.

Y la soltera aguarda, aguarda, aguarda.

Y no puede nacer en su hijo, en sus entrañas,
y no puede morir
en su cuerpo remoto, inexplorado,
planeta que el astrónomo calcula,
que existe aunque no ha visto.

Asomada a un cristal opaco la soltera
—astro extinguido— pinta con un lápiz
en sus labios la sangre que no tiene.

Y sonríe ante un amanecer sin nadie.

Woman Alone

To be an unmarried woman is shameful. All day
a feverish glow burns on her cheek.
(But the other cheek is eclipsed.)

The single woman busies herself with work of ashes,
in labors without merit and without issue;
at the hour when the family gathers
around the fire, when stories are read or told,
there is heard the cry
of a woman who shouts in an immense desert
where each rock, each scorched
trunk, each twisted
branch is a judge
or merciless witness.

At night the woman alone
stretches out on her agonized bed.
Sweat of anguish dampens the sheets
and the emptiness is peopled
with dialogues, with imagined men.

The unmarried woman waits, waits, waits.

She cannot be born in her child, in her womb,
nor can she die in her remote and unexplored body,
a planet whose existence
the astronomer has only surmised,
existing, although invisible.

Bending over opaque glass, the woman
(extinguished star) paints on her lips
the blood she is lacking.

And she smiles before an empty dawn.

Lívida luz

Apelación al solitario

Es necesario, a veces, encontrar compañía.

Amigo, no es posible ni nacer ni morir
sino con otro. Es bueno
que la amistad le quite
al trabajo esa cara de castigo
y a la alegría ese aire ilícito de robo.

¿Cómo podrías estar solo a la hora
completa, en que las cosas y tú hablan y hablan,
hasta el amanecer?

Appeal to the Solitary One

At times it behooves us to find companionship.

Friend, it's not possible to be born, or
to die, without the other. It is well
that friendship removes from work
that look of punishment, and from joy
the illicit air of theft.

How can you be alone at the total hour,
in which the things and you talk
and talk, til dawn?

Lívida luz

Destino

Matamos lo que amamos. Lo demás
no ha estado vivo nunca.
Ninguno está tan cerca. A ningún otro hiere
un olvido, una ausencia, a veces menos.
Matamos lo que amamos. ¡Que cese ya esta asfixia
de respirar con un pulmón ajeno!
El aire no es bastante
para los dos. Y no basta la tierra
para los cuerpos juntos
y la ración de la esperanza es poca
y el dolor no se puede compartir.

El hombre es animal de soledades,
ciervo con una flecha en el ijar
que huye y se desangra.

Ah, pero el odio, su fijeza insomne
de pupilas de vidrio; su actitud
que es a la vez reposo y amenaza.

El ciervo va a beber y en el agua aparece
el reflejo de un tigre.
El ciervo bebe el agua y la imagen. Se vuelve
—antes que lo devoren—(cómplice, fascinado)
igual a su enemigo.

Damos la vida sólo a lo que odiamos.

Destiny

We kill that which we love. The rest
was never alive.
No one is as close to us. No other is so hurt
by forgetfulness, an absence, a mere nothing.
We kill that which we love. An end to the asphyxia
of breathing with another's lungs!
The air isn't sufficient
for the two of us, nor the earth
for our bodies entwined.
The dose of hope is small
and sorrow cannot be shared.

Man is made of solitudes,
a deer in flight, bleeding,
its loins pierced by an arrow.

Ah, but hatred
its insomniac fixity of glass:
repose and menace combined.

The deer inclines its head to drink,
discovers a tiger's image in the water.
The deer drinks the water and its image. It becomes
(before it is devoured — astonished accomplice —)
equal to its enemy.

We give life only to what we hate.

Lívida luz

Lo cotidiano

Para el amor no hay cielo, amor, sólo este día;
este cabello triste que se cae
cuando te estás peinando ante el espejo.
Esos túneles largos
que se atraviesan con jadeo y asfixia;
las paredes sin ojos,
el hueco que resuena
de alguna voz oculta y sin sentido.

Para el amor no hay tregua, amor. La noche
no se vuelve, de pronto, respirable.
Y cuando un astro rompe sus cadenas
y lo ves zigzaguear, loco, y perderse,
no por ello la ley suelta sus garfios.
El encuentro es a oscuras. En el beso se mezcla
el sabor de las lágrimas.
Y en el abrazo ciñes
el recuerdo de aquella orfandad, de aquella muerte.

The Everyday

For love there is no heaven, love; only this day;
this sad strand of hair that falls
while you are combing before a mirror.
Those long tunnels
that we traverse panting and breathless;
the eyeless walls,
the emptiness that resounds with
some hidden and senseless voice.

For love there is no respite, love. The night
does not suddenly become bearable.
And when a star breaks its chains
and you see it madly zigzag, and disappear,
not for this does the law loosen its claws.
The encounter is in darkness. The taste
of tears mixes with the kiss.
And in the embrace you clasp the memory
of that orphanhood, of that death.

Lívida luz

Presencia

Algún día lo sabré. Este cuerpo que ha sido
mi albergue, mi prisión, mi hospital, es mi tumba.

Esto que uní alrededor de un ansia,
de un dolor, de un recuerdo,
desertará buscando el agua, la hoja,
la espora original y aun lo inerte y la piedra.

Este nudo que fui (inextricable
de cóleras, traiciones, esperanzas,
vislumbres repentinos, abandonos,
hambres, gritos de miedo y desamparo
y alegría fulgiendo en las tinieblas
y palabras y amor y amor y amores)
lo cortarán los años.

Nadie verá la destrucción. Ninguno
recogerá la página inconclusa.

Entre el puñado de actos
dispersos, aventados al azar, no habrá uno
al que pongan aparte como a perla preciosa.

Y sin embargo, hermano, amante, hijo,
amigo, antepasado,
no hay soledad, no hay muerte
aunque yo olvide y aunque yo me acabe.

Hombre, donde tú estás, donde tú vives
permanecemos todos.

Presence

Some day I'll know. This body that has been
my refuge, my prison, my hospital, is my tomb.

That which I gathered around a longing
for a grief, a memory,
will desert seeking water, a leaf,
the original spore and even the inert, a stone.

This knot that I was (inextricably composed
of anger, treasons, hopes,
sudden intimations, abandonments,
hungers, cries of fear and helplessness
and joy resplendent among the clouds
and words and love and love and loves)
the years will cut.

No one will see the destruction. No one
will pick up the unfinished page.

Among the handful of dispersed
actions, scattered to the wind, not one will be
set apart as a precious stone.

And yet, brother, lover, son
friend, ancestor
there is no solitude, no death
even if I forget and although I am no more.

Man, mankind, wherever you are, where you live
we — all of us — shall survive.

Lívida luz

Testamento de Hécuba

A Ofelia Guilmain, homenaje

Torre, no hiedra, fui. El viento nada pudo
rondando en torno mío con sus cuernos de toro:
alzaba polvaredas desde el norte y el sur
y aun desde otros puntos que olvidé o que ignoraba.
Pero yo resistía, profunda de cimientos,
ancha de muros, sólida
y caliente de entrañas, defendiendo a los míos.

El dolor era un deudo más de aquella familia.
No el predilecto ni el mayor. Un deudo
comedido en la faena, humilde comensal,
oscuro relator de cuentos junto al fuego.
Cazaba, en ocasiones, lejos, y por servir
su instinto de varón
que tiene el pulso firme y los ojos certeros.
Volvía con la presa y la entregaba al hábil
destazador y al diestro
afán de las mujeres.

Al recogerme yo decía: qué hermosa
labor están tejiendo con las horas mis manos.
Desde la juventud tuve frente a mis ojos
un hermoso dechado
y no ambicioné más que copiar su figura.
En su día fui casta
y después fiel al único, al esposo.

Nunca la aurora me encontró dormida
ni me alcanzó la noche
antes que se apagara mi rumor de colmena.
La casa de mi dueño se llenó de mis obras
y su campo llegó hasta el horizonte.

Hecuba's Testament

To Ofelia Guilmain, homage

I was a tower, not ivy. The circling wind
with its bulls' horns could not move me,
the wind that raised whirlwinds from the north and the south
and from other places I have forgotten.
But deeply-rooted, I endured,
massive-walled, firm
but passionately defending my own.

Grief was one more member of that family.
Not the first-born, not the favorite. A kinsman
content to work, austere at the table,
obscure teller of tales by the fire.
He would hunt, at times far off, to satisfy
the virile instincts of a man
who possesses a firm wrist, a sure eye.
He would return with the game and hand it over
to the skilled carver, to the women's
diligent hands.

Before sleeping I would say: what a splendid work
my hands are fashioning out of the hours.
From youth I kept a proud model
before my eyes,
my only ambition to emulate her figure.
In her time I was chaste,
afterwards faithful to my husband alone.

Dawn never surprised me sleeping
nor did night overtake me
before the bee-hum of my work was extinguished.
The house of my lord was filled with my labors
and his lands spanned the horizon.

Y para que su nombre no acabara
al acabar su cuerpo,
tuvo hijos en mí, valientes, laboriosos,
tuvo hijas de virtud,
desposadas con yernos aceptables
(excepto una, virgen, que se guardó a sí misma
tal vez como la ofrenda para un dios).

Los que me conocieron me llamaron dichosa
y no me contenté con recibir
la feliz alabanza de mis iguales
sino que me incliné hasta los pequeños
para sembrar en ellos gratitud.

Cuando vino el relámpago buscando
aquel árbol de las conversaciones
clamó por la injusticia el fulminado.

Yo no dije palabras, porque es condición mía
no entender otra cosa sino el deber y he sido
obediente al desastre:
viuda irreprensible, reina que pasó a esclava
sin que su dignidad de reina padeciera
y madre, ay, y madre
huérfana de su prole.

Arrastré la vejez como una túnica
demasiado pesada.
Quedé ciega de años y de llanto
y en mi ceguera vi
la visión que sostuvo en su lugar mi ánimo.

Vino la invalidez, el frío, el frío
y tuve que entregarme a la piedad
de los que viven. Antes
me entregué así al amor, al infortunio.

So that his name would survive
his body's release
I bore him sons, brave, long-toiling;
virtuous daughters
who found worthy husbands
(except one, a virgin, who kept to herself,
perhaps as an offering to a god).

My friends called me fortunate,
and not content with the praise of my equals
I bent down to the most humble
to sow gratitude among them.

When a lightning bolt sought
that tree of conversations,
the one who was stricken cried out against injustice.

I pronounced no words, because my condition
is to listen to duty alone;
so I have been obedient to disaster.
Irreproachable widow, enslaved queen who never
lost her regal bearing,
and mother, a mother orphaned
of her children.

I wore old age like a tunic
too heavy for my shoulders.
Blinded by years and weeping,
and in my blindness I saw
a vision that held my spirit at its center.

Then came infirmity, the cold, the cold,
and I had to submit to the pity
of the living. Before,
I submitted thus to love, to misfortune.

Alguien asiste mi agonía. Me hace
beber a sorbos una docilidad difícil
y yo voy aceptando
que se cumplan en mí los últimos misterios.

Someone comforts my agony
who makes me sip drops of harsh docility
and I slowly consent
to the consummation, within me,
of the final mysteries.

Materia memorable

Nota roja

En página primera
viene, como a embestir, este retrato
y luego, a ocho columnas, la noticia:
asesinado misteriosamente.

Es tan fácil morir, basta tan poco.
Un golpe a medianoche, por la espalda,
y aquí está ya el cadáver
puesto entre las mandíbulas de un público antropófago.

Mastica lentamente el nombre, las señales,
los secretos guardados con años de silencio,
la lepra oculta, el vicio nunca harto.

Del asesino nadie sabe nada:
cara con antifaz, mano con guantes.

Pero este cuerpo abierto en canal, esta entraña derramada en
                el suelo
hacen subir la fiebre
de cada Abel que mira su alrededor, temblando.

Scandal Sheet

On the front page
like an assault, appears
this photo, then, in eight columns, the news:
murder unsolved.

It's so easy to die, so little is needed.
A blow from behind at midnight
and there you have a corpse
placed conveniently between the jaws
            of a cannibal public,

which slowly chews the name, description,
secrets kept for years in silence,
the hidden corruption, insatiable vice.

Nothing is known of the assassin:
masked face, gloved hands.

But this body split wide open, these guts on the
        ·   sidewalk
raise the blood pressure
of every Abel of us who looks around him, trembling.

Materia memorable

Recordatorio

Obedecí, señores, las consignas.

Hice la reverencia a la entrada,
bailé los bailes de la adolescente
y me senté a aguardar el arribo del príncipe.

Se me acercaron unos con ese gesto astuto
y suficiente, del chalán de feria;
otros me sopesaron
para fijar el monto de mi dote
y alguien se fio del tacto de sus dedos
y así saber la urdimbre de mi entraña.

Hubo un intermediario entre mi cuerpo y yo,
un intérprete — Adán, que me dio el nombre
de mujer, que hoy ostento —
trazando en el espacio la figura
de un delta bifurcándose.

Ah, destino, destino.

He pagado el tributo de mi especie
pues di a la tierra, al mundo, esa criatura
en que se glorifica y se sustenta.

Es tiempo de acercarse a las orillas,
de volver a los patios interiores,
de apagar las antorchas
porque ya la tarea ha sido terminada.

Sin embargo, yo aún permanezco en mi sitio.

Señores, ¿no olvidasteis
dictar la orden de que me retire?

Reminder

Gentlemen, I obeyed your orders.

I bowed on entering,
I danced the adolescent dances,
and then sat down to wait for the arrival of the Prince.

Some approached me with the smug,
astute gesture of the horsedealer;
others calculated my weight
to judge the sum of my dowry
and another confided in his fingers' touch
to learn the warp of my internal organs.

There was an intermediary between me and my body
an interpreter—Adam, who gave me the name
of woman which I now bear—
tracing in space the figure
of a forking delta.

Ah, destiny, destiny.

I have paid the tribute of my species
because I gave the earth, the world, that child
in which it is nourished and glorified.

It's time to approach the shore,
to return to the inner patios,
to extinguish the torches
because the task has been accomplished.

However, I still remain in my place.

Gentlemen, have you forgotten
to order my withdrawal?

Materia memorable

Válium 10

A veces (y no trates
de restarle importancia
diciendo que no ocurre con frecuencia)
se te quiebra la vara con que mides,
se te extravía la brújula
y ya no entiendes nada.

El día se convierte en una sucesión
de hechos incoherentes, de funciones
que vas desempeñando por inercia y por hábito.

Y lo vives. Y dictas el oficio
a quienes corresponde. Y das la clase
lo mismo a los alumnos inscritos que al oyente.
Y en la noche redactas el texto que la imprenta
devorará mañana.
Y vigilas (oh, sólo por encima)
la marcha de la casa, la perfecta
coordinación de múltiples programas
—porque el hijo mayor ya viste de etiqueta
para ir de chambelán a un baile de quince años
y el menor quiere ser futbolista y el de en medio
tiene un póster del Che junto a su tocadiscos—.

Y repasas las cuentas del gasto y reflexionas,
junto a la cocinera, sobre el costo
de la vida y el ars magna combinatoria
del que surge el menú posible y cotidiano.

Y aún tienes voluntad para desmaquillarte
y ponerte la crema nutritiva y aún leer
algunas líneas antes de consumir la lámpara.

Valium 10

At times (and don't try
to make light of it saying
it doesn't happen often)
your measure breaks
the compass goes wild
and you can't make sense out of anything.

Your day turns into a succession
of incomprehensible actions, functions
which you fulfill out of inertia or habit.

And you live it. You dictate the letter
to Whom it concerns. You teach your class
to both auditors and regularly enrolled students.
And at night you prepare the text
the press will devour tomorrow.
And you watch over (oh, on top of everything else)
the running of a household, the perfect
coordination of multiple programs—because the eldest son
needs a tux for a coming-out party
the youngest wants to play soccer and the middle one
has a poster of Che beside the record player.

And you review the week's budget and reflect,
with the cook, on the cost of living
and the ars magna combinatoria
that produces the daily, the possible menu.

And you still have strength to remove your makeup
put on coldcream and even read
a few lines before exhausting the lamp.

Y ya en la oscuridad, en el umbral del sueño,
echas de menos lo que se ha perdido:
el diamante de más precio, la carta
de marear, el libro
con cien preguntas básicas (y sus correspondientes
respuestas) para un diálogo
elemental siquiera con la Esfinge.

Y tienes la penosa sensación
de que en el crucigrama se deslizó una errata
que lo hace irresoluble.

Y deletreas el nombre del Caos. Y no puedes
dormir si no destapas
el frasco de pastillas y si no tragas una
en la que se condensa,
químicamente pura, la ordenación del mundo.

In the darkness, on the edge
of sleep, you miss what was lost:
the most precious diamond, the navigation
chart, the book
of the Hundred Basic Questions (and their answers)
for an elementary dialogue with the Sphinx.

And you have the painful sensation
that an error slipped into the crossword puzzle
that makes a solution impossible.

And you spell out the name of Chaos. And
you can't go to sleep unless you open
the bottle of pills and take one
in which is condensed, chemically
pure, the world's order.

En la tierra de en medio

Se habla de Gabriel

Como todos los huéspedes mi hijo me estorbaba
ocupando un lugar que era mi lugar,
existiendo a deshora,
haciéndome partir en dos cada bocado.

Fea, enferma, aburrida
lo sentía crecer a mis expensas,
robarle su color a mi sangre, añadir
un peso y un volumen clandestinos
a mi modo de estar sobre la tierra.

Su cuerpo me pidió nacer, cederle el paso,
darle un sitio en el mundo,
la provisión de tiempo necesaria a su historia.

Consentí. Y por la herida en que partió, por esa
hemorragia de su desprendimiento
se fue también lo último que tuve
de soledad, de yo mirando tras de un vidrio.

Quedé abierta, ofrecida
a las visitaciones, al viento, a la presencia.

Speaking of Gabriel

Like all guests my son disturbed me
occupying a place that was mine
inopportunely,
obliging me to share each mouthful.

Ugly, sick, bored
I felt him grow at my expense,
steal his color from my blood, add
secret weight and volume
to my mode of being on the earth.

His body asked to be born, to make way for him,
to allow him a place in the sun,
the amount of time needed for his story.

I consented. And through that wound which bore
                    him, through that
hemorrhage of his release,
there departed as well the last trace
of my solitude, of looking through a glass.

I was left open, offering myself
to visitations, to the wind, to the presence.

En la tierra de en medio

Economía doméstica

He aquí la regla de oro, el secreto del orden:
tener un sitio para cada cosa
y tener
cada cosa en su sitio. Así arreglé mi casa.

Impecable anaquel el de los libros:
un apartado para las novelas,
otro para el ensayo
y la poesía en todo lo demás.

Si abres una alacena huele a espliego
y no confundirás los manteles de lino
con los que se usan cotidianamente.

Y hay también la vajilla de la gran ocasión
y la otra que se usa, se rompe, se repone
y nunca está completa.

La ropa en su cajón correspondiente
y los muebles guardando las distancias
y la composición que los hace armoniosos.

Naturalmente que la superficie
(de lo que sea) está pulida y limpia.
Y es también natural
que el polvo no se esconda en los rincones.

Pero hay algunas cosas
que provisionalmente coloqué aquí y allá
o que eché en el lugar de los trebejos.

Domestic Economy

Here's the golden rule, secret of domestic order:
to have a place for everything
and to have
everything in its place. So I arranged
my household.

A logical, impeccable bookcase:
a section for novels,
another for essay
and poetry in all the rest.

If you open a cupboard it smells of lavender
and there's no confusing the linen tablecloths
with those intended for daily use.

Also the set of dishes for the great occasion
and another set that's used, gets broken, is partially replaced
but is never quite complete.

Clothing arrayed in assigned drawers
and each piece of furniture keeping its distance,
a composition that makes for harmony.

Naturally the surfaces
(of whatever object) are clean, brightly polished.
Naturally also, dust is not allowed
to hide in the corners.

But there are some things
which I put here and there, for the moment,
or toss into a box of odds and ends.

Algunas cosas. Por ejemplo, un llanto
que no se lloró nunca;
una nostalgia de que me distraje,
un dolor, un dolor del que se borró el nombre,
un juramento no cumplido, un ansia
que se desvaneció como el perfume
de un frasco mal cerrado.

Y retazos de tiempo perdido en cualquier parte.

Esto me desazona. Siempre digo: mañana . . .
y luego olvido. Y muestro a las visitas,
orgullosa, una sala en la que resplandece
la regla de oro que me dio mi madre.

Some things. For example, a cry
that was never wept;
a nostalgia set aside,
a grief whose name was forgotten,
a promise unfulfilled, a desire
that disappeared like perfume
from a poorly closed bottle.

And remnants of time lost along the way.

All this makes me uncomfortable. I always say:
tomorrow. . .
and then forget. And I proudly show off to my guests
the sitting room where shines resplendent
the golden rule inherited from my mother.

En la tierra de en medio

Autorretrato[3]

Yo soy una señora: tratamiento
arduo de conseguir, en mi caso, y más útil
para alternar con los demás que un título
extendido a mi nombre en cualquier academia.

Así, pues, luzco mi trofeo y repito:
yo soy una señora. Gorda o flaca
según las posiciones de los astros,
los ciclos glandulares
y otros fenómenos que no comprendo.

Rubia, si elijo una peluca rubia.
O morena, según la alternativa.
(En realidad, mi pelo encanece, encanece.)

Soy más o menos fea. Eso depende mucho
de la mano que aplica el maquillaje.

Mi apariencia ha cambiado a lo largo del tiempo
—aunque no tanto como dice Weininger
que cambia la apariencia del genio—. Soy mediocre.
Lo cual, por una parte, me exime de enemigos
y, por la otra, me da la devoción
de algún admirador y la amistad
de esos hombres que hablan por teléfono
y envían largas cartas de felicitación.
Que beben lentamente whisky sobre las rocas
y charlan de política y de literatura.

Amigas . . . hmmm . . . a veces, raras veces
y en muy pequeñas dosis.
En general, rehuyo los espejos.
Me dirían lo de siempre: que me visto muy mal
y que hago el ridículo
cuando pretendo coquetear con alguien.

Self-Portrait[3]

I am a *señora*: a title difficult
to obtain (in my case) and more useful
for mingling with others than a degree
from an institution of higher learning.

Thus I show off my trophy and repeat:
I am a *señora*. Fat or thin, according
to the position of the stars
the glandular cycles and other
phenomena I do not understand.

Blonde, if I should choose a blonde wig.
Or dark, according to my moods.
(In truth, my hair is graying, graying.)

I am more or less ugly. But that depends
on the hand that applies the makeup.

My appearance has changed with the passage of time —
though not as much as Weininger said about
the changing appearance of genius —. I am mediocre.
That which, on the one hand, spares me enemies;
and on the other, assures me the devotion
of an admirer or two and the friendship
of men who speak incessantly on the telephone
and send long letters of congratulations.
Who slowly sip whiskey on the rocks
and talk of politics and literature.

Woman friends? Why, very seldom and in small
doses. As a rule I avoid mirrors.
As usual, they would tell me that I dress
badly, that I make a fool of myself
when I try to flirt with someone.

Soy madre de Gabriel: ya usted sabe, ese niño
que un día se erigirá en juez inapelable
y que acaso, además, ejerza de verdugo.
Mientras tanto lo amo.

Escribo. Este poema. Y otros. Y otros.
Hablo desde una cátedra.
Colaboro en revistas de mi especialidad
y un día a la semana publico en un periódico.

Vivo enfrente del Bosque. Pero casi
nunca vuelvo los ojos para mirarlo. Y nunca
atravieso la calle que me separa de él
y paseo y respiro y acaricio
la corteza rugosa de los árboles.

Sé que es obligatorio escuchar música
pero la eludo con frecuencia. Sé
que es bueno ver pintura
pero no voy jamás a las exposiciones
ni al estreno teatral ni al cine-club.

Prefiero estar aquí, como ahora, leyendo
y, si apago la luz, pensando un rato
en musarañas y otros menesteres.

Sufro más bien por hábito, por herencia, por no
diferenciarme más de mis congéneres
que por causas concretas.

Sería feliz si yo supiera cómo.
Es decir, si me hubieran enseñado los gestos,
los parlamentos, las decoraciones.

En cambio me enseñaron a llorar. Pero el llanto
es en mí un mecanismo descompuesto

I am Gabriel's mother: you know, that child
who will stand before me one day as a severe judge,
and besides, perhaps, may play the executioner.
Meanwhile, I love him.

I write. This poem. And others. And others.
I pontificate in front of my classes.
I contribute to journals of my specialty,
and, once a week, an article for a newspaper.

I live facing the park. But almost never
do I turn to look at it, nor do I cross
the street to stroll and breathe and
caress the trees' wrinkled skin.

I know it's obligatory to listen to music,
but I avoid it frequently. I know it's
fine to look at paintings
but I hardly ever go to art shows,
to the premières at the theater, or the ciné-club.

I prefer to remain here, as I am now,
reading and, if I turn off the light,
thinking of shadows and other trifles.

I suffer rather by habit, by tradition,
in order not to distinguish myself even more
from my compatriots than for specific reasons.

I would be happy, if I knew how.
That is, if they had taught me the gestures,
the speeches, the embellishments.

Instead they taught me how to weep.
But crying for me is a broken mechanism: I don't

y no lloro en la cámara mortuoria
ni en la ocasión sublime ni frente a la catástrofe.

Lloro cuando se quema el arroz o cuando pierdo
el último recibo del impuesto predial.

weep in front of the casket, on the sublime
occasion, or when faced by catastrophes.

I cry when I burn the rice or
when I lose the latest receipt for
the property taxes.

En la tierra de en medio

Narciso 70

Cuando abro los periódicos
(perdón por la inmodestia, pero a veces
un poco de verdad
es más alimenticia y confortante
que un par de huevos a la mexicana)
es para leer mi nombre escrito en ellos.

Mi nombre, que no abrevio por ninguna razón,
es, a pesar de todo, tan pequeño
como una anguila huidiza y se me pierde
entre las líneas ágata que si hablaban de mí
no recurrían más que al adjetivo neutro
tras el que se ocultaba mi persona, mi libro,
mi última conferencia.

¡Bah! ¡Qué importaba! ¡Estaba ahí! ¡Existía!
Real, patente ante mis propios ojos.

Pero cuando no estaba . . . Bueno, en fin,
hay que ensayar la muerte puesto que se es mortal.

Y cuando era una errata . . .

Narcissus 70

When I open a newspaper
(forgive, please, the lack of modesty
but at times a drop of truth
is more comforting and fortifying
than two fried eggs *a la mexicana*)
it's to see my name in print.

My name (that under no circumstances will I abbreviate)
is in spite of everything, as tiny
as a slippery eel that gets lost
among the agate lines, and if they spoke of me
they employed, alas, the indifferent adjective
behind which was hidden my person, my book,
my latest lecture.

Bah! What's the difference! I was there! I existed!
Patently real before my very eyes.

But when I wasn't . . . Well, we need
to try out death, because one is mortal.

And when there's an erratum . . .

En la tierra de en medio

Pequeña crónica

Entre nosotros hubo
lo que hay entre dos cuando se aman:
sangre del himen roto. (¿Te das cuenta?
Virgen a los treinta años ¡y poetisa! Lagarto.[4])

La hemorragia mensual o sea en la que un niño
dice que sí, dice que no a la vida.

Y la vena
—mía o de otra ¿qué más da?—en que el tajo
suicida se hundió un poco o lo bastante
como para volverse una esquela mortuoria.

Hubo, quizá, también otros humores:
el sudor del trabajo, el del placer,
la secreción verdosa de la cólera,
semen, saliva, lágrimas.

Nada, en fin, que un buen baño no borre. Y me pregunto
con qué voy a escribir, entonces, nuestra historia.
¿Con tinta? ¡Ay! Si la tinta
viene de tan ajenos manantiales.

Small Chronicle

Between us there was
what at times occurs between lovers:
blood of a torn hymen. (Can you imagine?
A virgin at thirty—and a poetess! Damn it.[4])

The monthly hemorrhage or that in which
a child says yes, says no to life.

And the vein
—mine or another's, what's the difference?—
into which the suicidal edge plunges
perhaps deeply enough to turn
one into a death notice.

There were, perhaps, other humors:
the sweat of work, that of pleasure,
anger's green secretion,
semen, saliva, tears.

In short, nothing a good bath
won't erase. And I wonder
with what, then, will I write our story?
With ink? Ah, but ink comes to us
from such distant sources.

En la tierra de en medio

Ajedrez

Porque éramos amigos y, a ratos, nos amábamos;
quizá para añadir otro interés
a los muchos que ya nos obligaban
decidimos jugar juegos de inteligencia.

Pusimos un tablero enfrente de nosotros:
equitativo en piezas, en valores,
en posibilidad de movimientos.
Aprendimos las reglas, les juramos respeto
y empezó la partida.

Henos aquí, hace un siglo, sentados, meditando
encarnizadamente
cómo dar el zarpazo último que aniquile
de modo inapelable y, para siempre, al otro.

Game of Chess

Because we were friends, and at times made love,
perhaps in order to add another interest
to the many that obliged us,
we decided to play games of the intellect.

We placed a board between us:
equal in pieces, in values,
in possibilities of movements.
We learned the rules, swore to observe them,
and so the game began.

Here we are, a century later, seated, meditating
frantically
on how to deliver the final blow that will
forever and inexorably annihilate the other.

En la tierra de en medio

Elegía

Nunca, como a tu lado, fui de piedra.

Y yo que me soñaba nube, agua,
aire sobre la hoja,
fuego de mil cambiantes llamaradas,
sólo supe yacer,
pesar, que es lo que sabe hacer la piedra
alrededor del cuello del ahogado.

Elegy

I was never so like a stone as when I was at your side.

I who dreamt I was a cloud, or water,
a breeze on a leaf,
fire of a thousand lambent tongues,
I only knew how to lie there,
to weigh heavily, which is what a stone
knows how to do
around a drowning man's neck.

En la tierra de en medio

Malinche[5]

Desde el sillón de mando mi madre dijo: "Ha muerto."

Y se dejó caer, como abatida,
en los brazos del otro, usurpador, padrastro
que la sostuvo no con el respeto
que el siervo da a la majestad de reina
sino con ese abajamiento mutuo
en que se humillan ambos, los amantes, los cómplices.

Desde la Plaza de los Intercambios
mi madre anunció: "Ha muerto."

La balanza
se sostuvo un instante sin moverse
y el grano de cacao quedó quieto en el arca
y el sol permanecía en la mitad del cielo
como aguardando un signo
que fue, cuando partió como una flecha,
el ay agudo de las plañideras.

"Se deshojó la flor de muchos pétalos,
se evaporó el perfume,
se consumió la llama de la antorcha.

Una niña regresa, escarbando, al lugar
en el que la partera depositó su ombligo.

Regresa al Sitio de los que Vivieron.

Reconoce a su padre asesinado,
ay, ay, ay, con veneno, con puñal,
con trampa ante sus pies, con lazo de horca.

Malinche[5]

From her royal throne my mother announced: "She is dead."

And then collapsed, humbled,
in the arms of the Other, the usurper, my stepfather
who sustained her not with the respect
a servant owes to the majesty of a queen
but with the mutual submissiveness
with which lovers, accomplices, abase themselves.

From the Plaza of the Changes
my mother announced: "She is dead."

The scale
remained immobile for an instant
the cacao bean reposed quietly in its chest
the sun stood still in the sky's zenith
as if awaiting a sign
which was, when it shot out like an arrow,
the penetrating cry of the mourners.

"The many-petaled flower has withered
the perfume has evaporated
the torch's flame extinguished.

A girlchild returns, scratching at
the spot where the midwife left her navel.

She returns to the Place of Those who have Lived.

She beholds her father, murdered,
woe, with poison, with a dagger,
with a trap, with a hangman's noose.

Se toman de la mano y caminan, caminan
perdiéndose en la niebla."

Tal era el llanto y las lamentaciones
sobre algún cuerpo anónimo; un cadáver
que no era el mío porque yo, vendida
a mercaderes, iba como esclava,
como nadie, al destierro.

Arrojada, expulsada
del reino, del palacio y de la entraña tibia
de la que me dio la luz en tálamo legítimo
y que me aborreció porque yo era su igual
en figura y en rango
y se contempló en mí y odió su imagen
y destrozó el espejo contra el suelo.

Yo avanzo hacia el destino entre cadenas
y dejo atrás lo que todavía escucho:
los fúnebres rumores con los que se me entierra.

Y la voz de mi madre con lágrimas ¡con lágrimas!
que decreta mi muerte.

Their hands touch and they walk, they walk,
disappearing into the fog."

Such was the weeping and lamentation
over an anonymous corpse; a cadaver
that was not mine, because I, sold to
the merchants, went forth to exile like a slave,
a pariah.

Expelled, cast out from
the kingdom, from the palace and warmth
of her who gave honest birth to me
and who despised me because I was her equal
in figure and rank
she who saw herself in me and hated her image
and dashed the mirror to the ground.

I go, in chains, toward my destiny
and am followed still by the sounds
of the mournful chants with which they bury me.

And the voice of my mother in tears—in tears!—
that decrees my death.

En la tierra de en medio

Ninfomanía

Te tuve entre mis manos:
la humanidad entera en una nuez.

¡Qué cáscara tan dura y tan rugosa!

Y, adentro, el simulacro
de los dos hemisferios cerebrales
que, obviamente, no aspiran a operar
sino a ser devorados, alabados
por ese sabor neutro, tan insatisfactorio
que exige, al infinito,
una vez y otra y otra, que se vuelva a probar.

Nymphomania

I had you in my grasp:
all of humanity in a nutshell.

What a hard and wrinkled rind!

And within, the simulacrum
of the two cerebral hemispheres
which, obviously, do not aspire to act upon
but to be devoured, lauded
for that neutral flavor, so unsatisfactory,
which demands of the infinite
to be tasted again and again, yet once more.

En la tierra de en medio

Entrevista de prensa

Pregunta el reportero, con la sagacidad
que le da la destreza de su oficio:
— ¿Por qué y para qué escribe?

— Pero, señor, es obvio. Porque alguien
(cuando yo era pequeña)
dijo que gente como yo, no existe.
Porque su cuerpo no proyecta sombra,
porque no arroja peso en la balanza,
porque su nombre es de los que se olvidan.
Y entonces . . . Pero no, no es tan sencillo.

Escribo porque yo, un día, adolescente,
me incliné ante un espejo y no había nadie.
¿Se da cuenta? El vacío. Y junto a mí los otros
chorreaban importancia.

No, no era envidia. Era algo más grave. Era otra cosa.
¿Comprende usted? Las únicas pasiones
lícitas a esa edad son metafísicas.
No me malinterprete.

Y luego, ya madura, descubrí
que la palabra tiene una virtud:
si es exacta es letal
como lo es un guante envenenado.

¿Quiere pasar a ver mi mausoleo?
¿Le gusta este cadáver? Pero si es nada más
una amistad inocua.
Y ésta una simpatía que no cuajó y aquél
no es más que un feto. Un feto.

Interview

The reporter asks, with the shrewdness
his profession has taught him:
"Why, to what purpose do you write?"

"Well, sir, it's obvious. Because someone
(when I was a small girl)
said that persons like myself do not exist.
Because their bodies cast no shadow,
because they register no weight on the scale,
because their names are to be forgotten.
And then. . . But no, it isn't that simple.

"I write because one day (I was an adolescent)
I looked in the mirror and no one was there.
Can you imagine? A void. And those
around me gushed importance.

"No, it wasn't envy. More serious than that. Something else.
Do you understand? The only legitimate passions
— at that age — are metaphysical.
Please don't misquote me.

"Then, later, a woman, I discovered
the power of the word:
when it's exact it's lethal
like a poisoned glove.

"Would you care to see my mausoleum?
How do you like that corpse? It's merely
an innocuous friendship.
And that one's a sympathy that didn't jell
and over there, a fetus. Just a fetus.

No me pregunte más. ¿Su clasificación?
En la tarjeta dice amor, felicidad,
lo que sea. No importa.
Nunca fue viable. Un feto en su frasco de alcohol.

Es decir, un poema
del libro del que usted hará el elogio.

"Don't ask more. Its classification?
On the card it says: love, happiness,
whatever. What's the difference.
It was never viable. A fetus kept
in alcohol. That is, a poem
from the book you'll one day praise."

En la tierra de en medio

Memorial de Tlatelolco[6]

La oscuridad engendra la violencia
y la violencia pide oscuridad
para cuajar en crimen.

Por eso el dos de octubre aguardó hasta la noche
para que nadie viera la mano que empuñaba
el arma, sino sólo su efecto de relámpago.

Y a esa luz, breve y lívida, ¿quién? ¿Quién es el que mata?
¿Quiénes los que agonizan, los que mueren?
¿Los que huyen sin zapatos?
¿Los que van a caer al pozo de una cárcel?
¿Los que se pudren en el hospital?
¿Los que se quedan mudos, para siempre, de espanto?

¿Quién? ¿Quiénes? Nadie. Al día siguiente, nadie.

La plaza amaneció barrida; los periódicos
dieron como noticia principal
el estado del tiempo.
Y en la televisión, en la radio, en el cine
no hubo ningún cambio de programa,
ningún anuncio intercalado ni un
minuto de silencio en el banquete.
(Pues prosiguió el banquete.)

No busques lo que no hay: huellas, cadáveres,
que todo se le ha dado como ofrenda a una diosa:
a la Devoradora de Excrementos.

No hurgues en los archivos pues nada consta en actas.

Memorial of Tlatelolco[6]

Darkness engenders violence
and violence wants darkness
to harden into crime.

Therefore the Second of October waited till the night
so that no one could see the hand that held
the weapon, only its bolt of lightning.

And in that light—brief, livid—who, *who* is it that kills?
Who are those that agonize, those that die?
Those that flee, bare feet, from the Plaza?
Those cast into a jail's pit?
Those who rot in a hospital?
Those left forever speechless out of fear?

Who? What persons? No one. The next day, no one.

The next morning the Plaza was swept clean;
the papers offered the weather
as the news of principal importance.
And on television, on the radio, in the movies,
there was no change of program
no newscast interruption
nor a moment of silence at the banquet
(the banquet went on as usual).

Don't look for what you won't find: traces, corpses,
since all was delivered up as an offering to a goddess:
the Devourer of Excrement.

Don't dig into the archives
because nothing is there recorded.

Ay, la violencia pide oscuridad
porque la oscuridad engendra el sueño
y podemos dormir soñando que soñamos.

Mas he aquí que toco una llaga: es mi memoria.
Duele, luego es verdad. Sangra con sangre.
Y si la llamo mía traiciono a todos.

Recuerdo, recordamos.

Esta es nuestra manera de ayudar que amanezca
sobre tantas conciencias mancilladas,
sobre un texto iracundo, sobre una reja abierta,
sobre el rostro amparado tras la máscara.

Recuerdo, recordemos
hasta que la justicia se siente entre nosotros.

Ah, violence wants darkness
because darkness engenders sleep
and we may sleep dreaming that we dream.

But suddenly I touch a wound: my memory.
It aches, therefore it's true. Bleeds with blood.
And if I call it mine alone I betray the others.

I remember, we remember.

This is our way of helping it to dawn
on so many defiled consciences,
on a raging text, on a gate flung open,
on a face hidden behind a mask.

I remember, may we remember
until justice sits once more among us.

En la tierra de en medio

Poesía no eres tú[7]

Porque si tú existieras
tendría que existir yo también. Y eso es mentira.

Nada hay más que nosotros: la pareja,
los sexos conciliados en un hijo,
las dos cabezas juntas, pero no contemplándose
(para no convertir a nadie en un espejo)
sino mirando frente a sí, hacia el otro.

El otro: mediador, juez, equilibrio
entre opuestos, testigo,
nudo en el que se anuda lo que se había roto.

El otro, la mudez que pide voz
al que tiene la voz
y reclama el oído del que escucha.

El otro. Con el otro
la humanidad, el diálogo, la poesía, comienzan.

Poetry Thou Art Not[7]

Because if you existed
my existence also were assured. And that is a lie.

There is nothing more than the two of us: the couple,
the two sexes reconciled in a child,
one head beside the other, but not contemplating one another
(let no one be a mirror)
but looking straight ahead, toward the other.

The other: mediator, judge, opposites
in equilibrium, witness,
knot which ties what had been torn.

The other, muteness that asks for voice
from its possessor
and demands hearing of him who listens.

The other. With the other
humanity, dialogue, poetry begin.

En la tierra de en medio

Kinsey Report

1

— ¿Si soy casada? Sí. Esto quiere decir
que se levantó un acta en alguna oficina
y se volvió amarilla con el tiempo
y que hubo ceremonia en una iglesia
con padrinos y todo. Y el banquete
y la semana entera en Acapulco.

No, ya no puedo usar mi vestido de boda.
He subido de peso con los hijos,
con las preocupaciones. Ya usted ve, no faltan.

Con frecuencia, que puedo predecir,
mi marido hace uso de sus derechos o,
como él gusta llamarlo, paga el débito
conyugal. Y me da la espalda. Y ronca.

Yo me resisto siempre. Por decoro.
Pero, siempre también, cedo. Por obediencia.

No, no me gusta nada.
De cualquier modo no debería de gustarme
porque yo soy decente ¡y él es tan material!

Además, me preocupa otro embarazo.
Y esos jadeos fuertes y el chirrido
de los resortes de la cama pueden
despertar a los niños que no duermen después
hasta la madrugada.

Kinsey Report

1

Married? Yes. That means
in some office a document was drawn up
that became yellow with age,
that there was a church wedding,
with best man and all the rest. Also a banquet
and an entire week in Acapulco.

My wedding dress doesn't fit anymore.
My weight has climbed what with children and their
problems. You see, there's no lack of them.

With a frequency that I can predict
my husband makes use of his rights,
or, as he likes to say, he performs his conjugal
duties. Then he turns his back. And snores.

I always resist, for decorum's sake.
But, too, I always submit. Out of obedience.

No, I don't like it in the least.
Anyway, I shouldn't like it because
I am a decent woman and he's so gross!

Besides, I'm concerned about another pregnancy.
And the loud panting and creaking of the bedsprings
may wake up the children,
who don't go to sleep again till dawn.

2

Soltera, sí. Pero no virgen. Tuve
un primo a los trece años.
El de catorce y no sabíamos nada.
Me asusté mucho. Fui con un doctor
que me dio algo y no hubo consecuencias.

Ahora soy mecanógrafa y algunas veces salgo
a pasear con amigos.
Al cine y a cenar. Y terminamos
la noche en un motel. Mi mamá no se entera.

Al principio me daba vergüenza, me humillaba
que los hombres me vieran de ese modo
después. Que me negaran
el derecho a negarme cuando no tenía ganas
porque me habían fichado como puta.

Y ni siquiera cobro. Y ni siquiera
puedo tener caprichos en la cama.

Son todos unos tales. ¿Que que por qué lo hago?
Porque me siento sola. O me fastidio.

Porque ¿no lo ve usted? estoy envejeciendo.
Ya perdí la esperanza de casarme
y prefiero una que otra cicatriz
a tener la memoria como un cofre vacío.

3

Divorciada. Porque era tan mula como todos.
Conozco a muchos más. Por eso es que comparo.

De cuando en cuando echo una cana al aire
para no convertirme en una histérica.

2

Unmarried, yes, but no virgin.
When I was thirteen a boy cousin and I . . .
He was fourteen and we were utterly ignorant.
I was scared. Went to a doctor who gave me
something and that was the end of it.

Now I am a secretary and at times go out with boyfriends,
a movie, supper; we always end up in a motel.
Mama knows nothing about it.

At first I was ashamed, it bothered me that men
should see me thus *afterward*, that they denied
me the right to refuse when I didn't feel like it,
because they decided I was a whore.

And I don't even charge, and can't even do what
I please in bed.

They're all bastards. Then why do I do it?
Because I'm lonely. Or bored.

It's that — don't you see — I'm getting old.
Lost all hope of marriage and
I'd rather have a scar or two
than a memory like an empty chest.

3

Divorced. Because he was a brute
like all the others. I've known all kinds,
that's why I can compare.

I take a fling from time to time
so I won't get hysterical.

Pero tengo que dar el buen ejemplo
a mis hijas. No quiero que su suerte
se parezca a la mía.

4

Tengo ofrecida a Dios esta abstinencia
¡por caridad, no entremos en detalles!

A veces sueño. A veces despierto derramándome
y me cuesta un trabajo decirle al confesor
que, otra vez, he caído porque la carne es flaca.

Y dejé de ir al cine. La oscuridad ayuda
y la aglomeración en los elevadores.

Creyeron que me iba a volver loca
pero me está atendiendo un médico. Masajes.

Y me siento mejor.

5

A los indispensables (como ellos se creen)
los puede usted echar a la basura,
como hicimos nosotras.

Mi amiga y yo nos entendemos bien.
Y la que manda es tierna, como compensación;
así como también, la que obedece,
es coqueta y se toma sus revanchas.

Vamos a muchas fiestas, viajamos a menudo
y en el hotel pedimos
un solo cuarto y una sola cama.

Se burlan de nosotras pero también nosotras
nos burlamos de ellos y quedamos a mano.

But I need to set a good example
for my daughters. I don't want their fate
to be like mine.

4

This abstinence is an offering to God.
For pity's sake, let's not go into details!

I dream at times. I wake up wet and it's
painful to tell my confessor that
I've sinned again because the flesh is weak.

I no longer go to movies. Darkness is
an accomplice, and the temptation of elevators.

They thought I was losing my mind,
but a physician is taking care of me. Massages.

I feel much better.

5

As for those indispensable persons (as
they think they are) you can throw them in
the trash can, as we did.

My girlfriend and I understand each other well.
The strong partner is gentle, by way of compensation;
the obedient one is a coquette, and
she gets even.

Certainly, we go to parties, we travel
and in hotels we ask for
one room and one bed.

They make fun of us but we
pay them with the same coin.

Cuando nos aburramos de estar solas
alguna de las dos irá a agenciarse un hijo.
¡No, no de esa manera! En el laboratorio
de la inseminación artificial.

6

Señorita. Sí, insisto. Señorita.

Soy joven. Dicen que no fea. Carácter
llevadero. Y un día
vendrá el Príncipe Azul, porque se lo he rogado
como un milagro a San Antonio. Entonces
vamos a ser felices. Enamorados siempre.

¿Qué importa la pobreza? Y si es borracho
lo quitaré del vicio. Si es un mujeriego
yo voy a mantenerme siempre tan atractiva,
tan atenta a sus gustos, tan buena ama de casa,
tan prolífica madre
y tan extraordinaria cocinera
que se volverá fiel como premio a mis méritos
entre los que, el mayor, es la paciencia.

Lo mismo que mis padres y los de mi marido
celebraremos nuestras bodas de oro
con gran misa solemne.

No, no he tenido novio. No, ninguno
todavía. Mañana.

When we get tired of living alone
one of us will manage to have a child.
No, not that way! By artificial insemination.

6

Señorita. Yes, I insist. *Señorita.*

I'm young and not bad looking.
Easy going. One day
my prince will turn up, because, you know,
I've prayed for a miracle to Saint Anthony.
We'll be happy, then, forever . . .

What if he *is* poor? If he drinks too
much I'll straighten him out.
If he turns out to be a woman chaser
well, I'll keep myself so attractive,
so attentive to his desires, so splendid a housewife,
such a prolific mother
and superb cook
that he'll be faithful in recognition
of my merits, among which the greatest is patience.

Just as my parents did, and his,
we'll celebrate our golden anniversary
with a *missa solemnis*.

No, I haven't had a boyfriend. None,
as yet. Tomorrow.

Otros poemas

Evocación de la tía Elena

La recuerdo viniendo hacia mi infancia
desde su hermoso mundo de cosméticos.
Toda la línea Arden sobre su tocador
y ella, pensativa, exigiéndole un voto
de confianza al espejo. El color de su tez,
la perfección de su perfil, el orden
de su pelo eran siempre materia cuestionada.

Más allá de la doble superficie
ponderaba otra cosa:
¿es lícito destruir la obra de la belleza
cuando sólo enmascara al sufrimiento?

Y ponía en la balanza el gramo de cianuro
que escondía entre sus joyas
para hacerla perder su equilibrio, inclinarse
del lado del destino.

Aunt Elena

I remember her converging on my childhood
from her brilliant world of cosmetics.
All the Arden line on her dressing table
and she, pensive, demanding a vote
of confidence from her mirror. The color of her
skin, her profile's perfection, her hair's
arrangement were always debatable matters.

Beyond that double surface
she pondered another problem:
is it licit to destroy a work of beauty
when it merely disguises suffering?

And she placed on the scale a gram of cyanide
hidden among her jewels
to make it lose its balance, to lean
toward the side of destiny.

Otros poemas

Acto de humildad

En otro tiempo me maravilló
lo fácil que era ser solamente una vaca.
Bastaba con echarse a rumiar y con parir
cada año un becerro. Con mirar sin asombro
la estructura del mundo y sus apariciones.
Con dejarse engordar y, mansamente,
ir con los otros hacia el matadero.

Es, en verdad, muy fácil. Pero si lo pensamos
con equidad tampoco es una proeza
ser . . . en fin . . . lo que somos.

Act of Humility

Long ago I was amazed
at how easy it was to be nothing more than a cow.
Ruminating was sufficient then, and the yearly issue of a new calf.
Or observing without surprise the structure
of the world and its phantoms.
Or letting oneself get fat and tamely
moving with the rest toward the slaughter.

Really, it is quite easy. But if
we consider the matter with equanimity
neither is it exactly heroic
to be that which . . . after all . . . we are.

Otros poemas

De mutilaciones

Un día dices: La uña. ¿Qué es la uña?
Una excrecencia córnea
que es preciso cortar. Y te la cortas.

Y te cortas el pelo para estar a la moda
y no hay en ello merma ni dolor.

Otro día viene Shylock y te exige
una libra de carne, de tu carne,
para pagar la deuda que le debes.

Y, después. Oh, después:
palabras que te extraen de la boca,
trepanación del cráneo
para extirpar ese tumor que crece
cuando piensas.

A la vista del recaudador
entregas, como ofrenda, tu parálisis.

Para tu muerte es excesivo un féretro
porque no conservaste nada tuyo
que no quepa en la cáscara de nuez.

Y epitafio ¿en qué lápida?
Ninguna es tan pequeña como para escribir
las letras que quedaron de tu nombre.

Mutilations

One day you say: the nail. What is a nail?
A hard excrescence
that must be pruned. And you clip it.

And you cut your hair to be in fashion
which causes neither pain nor loss.

Another day comes Shylock to demand
his pound of flesh, your flesh,
to satisfy your debt to him.

And afterwards. Oh, afterwards.
Words are extracted from your mouth,
trephination of the skull
to extirpate that tumor that grows
when you think.

When the tax-collector arrives
you turn over, as an offering, your paralysis.

A coffin is excessive for your death
because nothing of you is left
that wouldn't fit in a nutshell.

An epitaph, on what stone?
None is small enough to contain
the remaining letters of your name.

Otros poemas

Tan-tan, ¿Quién es?

Cuando toca tres veces San Pascual
responde el alma: no, todavía no.
Tengo una sopa a medio cocinar, un suéter
al que aún no termino las mangas, un asunto
pendiente de sentencia en el juzgado.

Y mis hijos que no quieren ser huérfanos
y el otro que no sabe enviudar. Y lo que falta.

Nunca me dieron suficiente tiempo
y ahora . . . No es mi culpa. Yo te suplico un plazo.

—¿Pero qué suponías que es la muerte
sino este llegar tarde a todas partes
y este dejar a medias cualquier cosa
y este sumar, restar, enredarse en los cálculos
y no contar con excedentes nunca?

La muerte, como todo lo humano, es la carencia,
el agotarse de los materiales
de que se estuvo hecho. El cambio de los signos
junto a las cantidades que figuran
en el Libro Mayor.

Representas un déficit, eres la cifra roja
y no extendemos créditos porque tal precedente
nos crearía problemas. Y, como ves, no hay nada
más simple que el negocio que estamos manejando.

Knock, Knock, Who's There?

When Saint Pascual knocks three times
the soul will answer: no, not yet.
I have a soup half-done, a sweater
still sleeveless, a matter
in the courts that needs to be settled.

Besides, my children don't care to be orphans, and *he*
won't know how to manage as a widower. And all the rest.

They never allowed me enough time
and . . . It's not my fault, please postpone the date.

"But what did you think death was
if not this always arriving late everywhere
leaving everything half done
and this adding, subtracting, confusing the figures,
never counting on a surplus?

"Death, like all things human, is a lack,
a using up of the materials
of which one was made. A change of
signs beside the quantities that figure
in the great Reckoning.

"You are a deficit, you're in the red
and we don't extend credit because
such a precedent would create problems.
So, as you see, there is nothing simpler
than this business in which we are engaged."

Otros poemas

Ninguneo

En la tierra de Descartes, junto a la estufa
—ya que nieva y tirito—
no pienso, pues pensar no es mi fuerte; ni siento
pues mi especialidad no es sentir sino sólo
mirar, así que digo:
(pues la palabra es la mirada fija)
¿qué diablos hago aquí en la Ciudad Lux,
presumiendo de culta y de viajada
sino aplazar la ejecución de una
sentencia que ha caído sobre mí?

La sentencia que dicta: "No existes." Y la firman
los que para firmar usan el Nos
mayestático: el Unico que es Todos;
los magistrados, las cancillerías,
las altas partes contratantes, los
trece emperadores aztecas, los poderes
legislativo y judicial, la lista
de Virreyes, la Comisión de Box,
los institutos descentralizados
el Sindicato Unico de Voceadores y . . .
. . . y, solidariamente, mis demás compatriotas.

Anéantissement

In the land of Descartes, next to the heater
(it's snowing and I'm shivering)
I do not think, because thinking isn't my strong
point, nor do I feel
because my specialty is not feeling, but only
looking. So I say
(since the word and the look are one):
what the devil am I doing here in the City of Light
presuming to possess culture and the refinements of travel
when it's simply a case of postponing
the execution of a sentence read over my person?

A sentence which states: "You do not exist."
Signed by those who employ the regal We;
the One that is All; the magistrates,
chancelleries, the major contracting parties,
the Thirteen Aztec Emperors, the judicial
and legislative branches, the list
of Viceroys, the Boxing Commission,
the Decentralized Colleges,
the Single Union of Newspaper Hawkers
. . . and, out of solidarity, the rest of my countrymen.

Viaje redondo

Pasaporte

¿Mujer de ideas? No, nunca he tenido una.
Jamás repetí otras (por pudor o por fallas nemotécnicas).
¿Mujer de acción? Tampoco.
Basta mirar la talla de mis pies y mis manos.

Mujer, pues, de palabra. No, de palabra no.
Pero sí de palabras,
muchas, contradictorias, ay, insignificantes,
sonido puro, vacuo cernido de arabescos,
juego de salón, chisme, espuma, olvido.

Pero si es necesaria una definición
para el papel de identidad, apunte
que soy mujer de buenas intenciones
y que he pavimentado
un camino directo y fácil al infierno.

Passport

Woman of ideas? I've never had one.
Nor did I ever repeat those of others (from modesty or lack of
        skill in mnemotechnics).
Woman of action? Hardly. Consider the size
of my hands and feet.

Woman, then, of a word. No, not of a word.
Rather, of words,
many, contradictory, insignificant,
pure sound, vacancy sprinkled with arabesques,
parlor games, gossip, froth, forgetfulness.

But if a definition is required
for purposes of identification,
put down a woman of good intention
who has paved
a straight and easy road to hell.

Viaje redondo

Encargo

Cuando yo muera dadme la muerte que me falta
y no me recordéis.
No repitáis mi nombre hasta que el aire sea
transparente otra vez.

No erijáis monumentos que el espacio que tuve
entero lo devuelvo a su dueño y señor
para que advenga el otro, el esperado
y resplandezca el signo del favor.

Request

When I die give me the death that is befitting
and don't remember me
don't repeat my name until the air is clear again.

Do not erect monuments, since I give back the space
I occupied to its lord and master,
so that the Other may come, the Awaited,
that the emblem of fortune may shine forth.

Materia memorable

Note on the Translations

The great majority of Castellanos' poems are written in free verse, and therefore offer no difficulty to the translator with regard to meter and rhyme. However, in her best poems, those that seem entirely conversational and colloquial in form and tone like "Valium 10," there are occasional nuances, ambiguities, colloquial allusions and turns of phrase which offer thorny problems to the translator: their simplicity is highly deceptive. I have sought to retain the sense at all times without sacrificing normal English constructions and syntax. When that was not possible, I have added an explanatory note, as in the case of *lagarto* in "Small Chronicle."

Notes

[1] Clemencia Isaura was a "Frenchwoman from Toulouse, born and died during the fifteenth century, whose existence is in some doubt, to whom is attributed the spread, and, mistakenly, the creation of the Flower Game festivals of the city of Toulouse." From the *Enciclopedia Universal Ilustrada*, Espasa-Calpe, 1926. The "Flower Games" were poetry contests, a tradition which still persists in some Latin countries.

[2] See the translator's introduction for a discussion of this poem.

[3] See the discussion of this poem in the translator's introduction.

[4] The word *lagarto* (lizard, l. 4 of the Spanish original) used in this context is an exclamation that derives from a popular superstition: that seeing a reptile is bad luck, but one can ward off the evil by pronouncing *lagarto*. English is unable to convey the ironically superstitious tone of the expression. We have decided to use a simple expletive that conveys displeasure (damn it).

[5] The poem does not narrate the best known aspects of the life of the Indian princess (also known as Marina) who became mistress, interpreter, and advisor to Hernán Cortés and whose cooperation was crucial to the conquest of Mexico; rather, it goes back to her origins, how she was sold to a chief of Tabasco. "She was the daughter of a powerful *cacique*, lord of many municipalities and feudatory of the Mexican empire. Upon his death, her mother, who was left a widow at a young age, married again and had a son by this second marriage. The love for her son made her begin to hate her daughter, to the point of making her devise an evil scheme. Taking advantage of the death of the daughter of one of her slaves, of the same age as Marina, she made it known that her own daughter had died, and she buried the girl's body with all the honors due a young woman of her rank. Meanwhile, poor Marina had been sold to slave dealers from Ficallanco, a city near Tabasco; and the latter sold her to the *cacique* of Tabasco, who presented her, along with others, to Cortés, in order to prepare the troop's corn." *Enciclopedia Espasa-Calpe*, 1926, under the name "Marina." This episode recalls Rosario Castella-

nos' novel *Balún Canán*, in which a male sibling was also preferred over his sister.

⁶ On October 2, 1968, during the Mexican Olympics, a group of police or army (it has never been ascertained exactly who was responsible) fired on a large mass of peaceful demonstrators in the closed square of Tlatelolco, or the *Plaza de las Tres Culturas*, in Mexico City. News of the event was suppressed by the government, and the number of dead, never officially revealed, varies from 100 to 400 depending on the source. Octavio Paz (*Posdata*) and Elena Poniatowska have published books on the subject.

⁷ The title alludes to a lyric by the romantic poet Gustavo Adolfo Bécquer (Spain, 1836–1870), *Poesía eres tú*. The first lines are a paraphrase of a statement by the philosopher Unamuno which affirms that man's existence and immortality depend upon that of God. The rest of the poem seems to assert that poetry can only be born out of dialogue with some *other*: lover, friend, reader.

Selected Bibliography

For the most complete bibliography to 1980, see Maureen Ahern and Mary Seale Vázquez, eds., *Homenaje a Rosario Castellanos*. Valencia: Ediciones Albatros-Hispanófila, 1980.

Poetry

Trayectoria del polvo. México: Colección El Cristal Fugitivo, 1948.
Apuntes para una declaración de fe. México: Ediciones de América, 1948.
De la vigilia estéril. México: Ediciones de "América," 1950.
Dos poemas. México: Icaro, 1950.
El rescate del mundo. México: Ediciones de América, 1952.
Poemas (1953–1955). México: Colección Metáfora, 1957.
Salomé y Judith: Poemas dramáticos. México: Editorial Jus, 1959.
Al pie de la letra. Xalapa: Universidad Veracruzana, 1959.
Lívida luz. México: Universidad Nacional Autónoma de México, 1960.
Materia memorable. México: Universidad Nacional Autónoma de México, 1969.
Poesía no eres tú: Obra poética: 1948–1971. 1st ed., México: Fondo de Cultura Económica, 1972. 2nd ed., 1975. Poems collected from all the above editions, with the addition of four collections written after 1969: *En la tierra de en medio*, *Diálogos con los hombres más honrados*, *Otros poemas*, and *Viaje redondo*. Included also are translations from Emily Dickinson, St.-John Perse, and Paul Claudel.

Narrative

Balún Canán (novel). México: Fondo de Cultura Económica, 1957.
Ciudad Real: Cuentos. Xalapa: Universidad Veracruzana, 1960.
Oficio de tinieblas (novel). México: Joaquín Mortiz, 1962.
Los convidados de agosto (short stories). México: Ediciones Era, 1964.
Album de familia (short stories). México: Joaquín Mortiz, 1971. Includes "Lección de cocina."

Theatre

"Tablero de damas: Pieza en un acto." *América: Revista Antológica*, No. 68 (June 1952), 185–224.
"Petul en la Escuela Abierta." In *Teatro Petul*. México: Instituto Nacional Indigenista, n.d., 1962, pp. 42–65.
El eterno femenino: farsa. México: Fondo de Cultura Económica, 1975.

Essays

Juicios sumarios: ensayos. Xalapa: Universidad Veracruzana, 1966.
Mujer que sabe latín . . . México: Secretaría de Educación Pública, 1973. (SepSetentas, 83.)

El uso de la palabra. Prologue by José Emilio Pacheco. México: Ediciones de Excélsior-Crónicas, 1974.

El mar y sus pescaditos. México: Secretaría de Educación Pública, 1975. (SepSetentas, 89.)

Selected Critical Bibliography

A Rosario Castellanos, sus amigos. Publ. especial del Año Internacional de la Mujer. México: Cía. Impresora y Litografía Juventud, 1975.

Ahern, Maureen and Mary Seale Vázquez, eds., *Homenaje a Rosario Castellanos.* Valencia: Ediciones Albatros-Hispanófila, 1980.

Alvarez, Griselda. *Diez mujeres en la poesía mexicana del siglo XX.* México: Col. Metropolitana, 1973.

Baptiste, Víctor. *La obra poética de Rosario Castellanos.* Santiago de Chile: Ed. Exégesis, 1972. Diss. University of Illinois, 1967.

Bigelow, Marcia Anne. "La evolución de la hablante en la poesía de Rosario Castellanos." Diss. University of California, Irvine, 1984.

Calderón, Germaine. *El universo poético de Rosario Castellanos.* México: UNAM, Centro de Estudios Literarios, 1979.

Carballo, Emmanuel. "Rosario Castellanos. La historia de sus libros contada por ella misma." *La cultura en México,* Supl. of *Siempre!,* 44, 19 dic., 1962, pp. II-V. Also in his *Diecinueve protagonistas de la literatura mexicana del siglo XX.* México: Empresas Editoriales, 1965, pp. 411-424.

Castro Leal, Antonio. "Dos poemas dramáticos en *Poesía no eres tú.*" *Vida Literaria,* No. 30, 5, 6.

Dabdoub, Mary Lou. "Ultima charla con Rosario Castellanos." *Revista de Revistas,* 119, 11 sept., 1974, pp. 44-46.

De Beer, Gabriella. "Feminismo en la obra poética de Rosario Castellanos." *Revista de Crítica Literaria Latinoamericana* (Lima), 7 (1981), No. 13, 95-112.

Fiscal, María Rosa. *La imagen de la mujer en la narrativa de Rosario Castellanos.* México: UNAM, Centro de Estudios Literarios, 1980.

Frenk Alatorre, Margit. "Sobre cultura femenina." *México en la Cultura,* supl. of *Novedades,* 97, 10 dic., 1950, p. 7. (Review of Castellanos' published thesis, *Sobre cultura femenina.*)

García Flores, Margarita. "Rosario Castellanos: la lucidez como forma de vida." *La onda,* supl. of *Novedades,* 149, 19 agosto, 1974, 6, 7.

Labastida, Jaime. *El amor, el sueño y la muerte en la poesía mexicana.* México, 1974.

Miller, Beth. "Voz e imagen en la obra de Rosario Castellanos." *Revista de la Universidad de México,* 30, 4 (1975-76), 33-38. Also in her *Mujeres en la literatura.* México: Fleischer Editora, 1978, pp. 9-19.

———. "La poesía de Rosario Castellanos: tono y tenor." *Diálogos,* 2, 13 (marzo-abril 1977), 28-31.

———. "Woman and Feminism in the Works of Rosario Castellanos." In *Feminist Criticism: Essays on Theory, Poetry and Prose.* Eds. Cheryl L. Brown and Karen Olson. Metuchen and London: Scarecrow Press, 1978, pp. 198-210.

————. *Rosario Castellanos: Una conciencia femenina en México.* Chiapas: Univ. Autónoma de Chiapas, 1983.

Miller, Yvette E. "El temario poético de Rosario Castellanos." *Hispamérica*, 29, X, No. 29, 107-115.

Pacheco, José Emilio. "Rosario Castellanos o la rotunda austeridad de la poesía." *Vida Literaria*, 30 (1972), 8-11.

————. "Rosario Castellanos o la literatura como ejercicio de la libertad." *Diorama de la Cultura*, supl. of *Excélsior*, 11 agosto, 1974, p. 16. Also as "La palabra. Nota preliminar." In Rosario Castellanos, *El uso de la palabra*. México: Ediciones de Excélsior-Crónicas, 1974, pp. 7-13.

Poniatowska, Elena. "Evocaciones de Rosario Castellanos." *Cultura en México*, supl. of *Siempre!*, No. 1106, 4 sept., 1974, 6-8.

Rebolledo, Tey Diana. "The Wind and the Tree: A Structural Analysis of the Poetry of Rosario Castellanos." Diss. University of Arizona, 1979.

Rivero, Eliana. "Visión social y feminista en la obra poética de Rosario Castellanos." In Ahern and Seale Vázquez, *Homenaje* . . . pp. 85-97.

Seale Vázquez, Mary. "Rosario Castellanos: Image and Idea." In Ahern and Seale Vázquez, *Homenaje* . . . pp. 15-40.